LOOKING TOWARDS

WEST SUSSEX COUNTRY CHURCHES

ST. GILES, GRAFFHAM.

DETAILED DRAWINGS BY EDWIN WILKINSON

DEDICATION

This book is dedicated, with enormous gratitude, to those who express their personal faith and worship within our ancient churches, and in so doing preserve an impressive heritage in our national culture.

ACKNOWLEDGEMENTS

To the clergy and churchwardens of these churches for their provision of information and willingness to assist my project. To the staff at the Chichester Diocesan Records Office, and West Sussex Record Office. The Yale University Press for permission to use the item from Nairn Pevsner's *The Buildings of England – Sussex*. To my wife and sister-in-law for their endeavours when assistance was called for. To friends for their interest and encouragement along the way.

First published in 2003 by S B Publications
19 Grove Road, Seaford, East Sussex BN25 1TP
telephone: 01323 893498
fax: 01323 893860
email: sbpublications@tiscali.co.uk

ISBN 185770 277 8

Typeset by JEM Editorial, JEMedit@AOL.com
Printed by Pageturn Ltd, East Sussex, BN3 7EG. Tel: (01273) 821500

Front cover: Fittleworth, St Mary
Back cover: Graffham, lych gate at St Giles

CONTENTS

Foreword 4

Introduction 5

Churches:

Aldingbourne, St Mary the Virgin 62

Amberley, St Michael 90

Angmering, St Margaret 42

Barlavington, St Mary 18

Barnham, St Mary 82

Bepton, St Mary 84

Billingshurst, St Mary 30

Binsted, St Mary 80

Bosham, Holy Trinity 66

Boxgrove Priory 72

Burpham, St Mary the Virgin 40

Bury, St John the Evangelist 100

Church Norton, St Wilfrid 6

Clymping, St Mary 56

Cocking (no dedication) 58

Coldwaltham, St Giles 54

Cowfold, St Peter 44

Didling, St Andrew 8

Donnington, St George 86

Eastergate, St George 46

East Lavant, St Mary 88

Elsted, St Paul 38

Findon, St John the Baptist 68

Ford, St Andrew 60

Funtington, St Mary 92

Harting, St Mary & St Gabriel 64

Heyshott, St James 34

Kirdford, St John the Baptist 50

Lurgashall, St Laurence 22

Lyminster, St Mary Magdalene 14

North Mundham, St Stephen 26

Poling, St Nicholas 16

Sennicotts, St Mary 78

Shipley, St Mary the Virgin 76

Sompting, St Mary the Virgin 96

Stedham, St James 70

Steyning, St Andrew 94

Storrington, St Mary 48

Sutton, St John the Baptist 32

Tillington, All Hallows 98

Trotton, St George 24

Walberton, St Mary 12

West Chiltington, St Mary 10

West Grinstead, St George 52

West Stoke, St Andrew 74

West Wittering, St Peter & St Paul 20

Wisborough Green, St Peter ad Vincula 28

Yapton, St Mary the Virgin 36

Reference map 102

FOREWORD

by Lord Harris of High Cross

The reader of this charming book might not easily credit that the drawings are the work of an amateur artist whom I have been privileged to know as a gifted preacher at St Andrew's Church, Jevington in East Sussex. And yet his meticulous craftsmanship conveys the same love and dedication as his joyful sermons.

For me, as an economist, not the least wonder is that this shared heritage, in all its rich diversity going back to Saxon times, owes nothing to support from the public purse. Do let us all remember that when next confronted with a church collection plate or an appeal to maintain the precious fabric of these ancient buildings.

Ralph Harris

INTRODUCTION

These drawings of fifty West Sussex country churches follow a similar publication of some years ago, illustrating all the Rye Deanery churches. Ancient church buildings inevitably reflect something of the social, theological and architectural changes of the generations, hence the fascination leading to the presentation of these drawings and information. Not that I claim to represent each church to fullest degree, far from it, there will always be much more for the interested visitor to look for and find, but I have responded as each church appealed to me from an artist's point of view. Other buildings of interest have been included in a few instances, simply because in visiting the one the other was virtually unavoidable and, of course, had artistic appeal.

My interest in ancient churches stems largely from a period as vicar of a church with Saxon origins. In the event I find myself again worshipping in a church where congregations have gathered spanning a thousand years, and where the Saxon parts are still obvious in the overall architecture of the building. What changes the wider Church has seen during this, the second millennium. From Celtic beginnings to Roman mission, from Anglo-Saxon to Norman, from the Crusades to Renaissance and Reformation and on to the Elizabethan Settlement. Through the Civil War and influence of the Counter Reformation, to Georgian neglect and Victorian renewal. The parts and influences of these movements can be detected, in greater or lesser degree, in the fabric of our ancient churches.

The introduction of the Book of Common Prayer in the reign of Edward VI, and the Religious Settlement under Queen Elizabeth I, effectively 'Anglicised' the Church, making it 'the people's Church', the Church for the English nation, its ministries available to all citizens. The whole nation was sub-divided into areas called parishes, each parish having a church to serve the population, hence the title 'parish church'. Basically that system remains intact today, and it is worth bearing in mind that the churches here illustrated are places where people still gather for worship and fellowship in the Word and Sacraments as their predecessors have done for centuries, they partake in a chain of prayer, a spiritual succession, to which the very stones of these buildings are witness.

Exploring these churches has been a great pleasure and increased my already deep admiration for those who, with care and devotion, preserve the continuity of this part of our Christian and national heritage.

Edwin Wilkinson

St Wilfrid, Church Norton, Selsey.

Church Norton, St Wilfrid

From the B road turn off to Church Norton, half a mile north of Selsey. St Wilfrid's is virtually a 'cemetery chapel', all that remains of a larger twelfth-thirteenth century building, the nave of which was pulled down in the mid-nineteenth century. Materials from the old church, such as the pillars, arches and font, were incorporated into the building of St Peter's, Selsey, in 1865. St Wilfrid's, and the large cemetery, are in the parish of St Peter. In 1917 the Bishop of Chichester dedicated the chapel to St Wilfrid, who founded a monastery at Selsey in 686AD, the beginning of what was to become Chichester Cathedral. His personal chaplain was Eddius Stephanus, hence the association in the chapel with Rudyard Kipling's poem, *Eddi's Service*. The nearby shingle beach, and parish church of St Peter, will add to the visitor's pleasure and interest while in the area.

A beautifully crafted white marble statue stands alongside the church east wall in memory of Stephanie Agnes Wingfield, of Norton Priory, who died on December 9, 1918. The complimentary inscription on the memorial reads:

Green be the turf above thee,
Friend of my better days,
None knew thee but to love thee,
Nor named thee but to praise.

Eddi's Service

Eddi, priest of St Wilfrid
In his chapel at Manhood End,
Ordered a midnight service
For such as cared to attend

But the Saxons were keeping Christmas,
And the night was stormy as well.
Nobody came to the service
Though Eddi rang the bell.

'Wicked weather for walking,'
Said Eddi of Manhood End,
'But I must go on with the service
For such as care to attend.'

The altar lamps were lighted –
An old marsh-donkey came,
Bold as a guest invited
And stared at the guttering flame.

The storm beat on the windows,
The water splashed on the floor,
And a wet, yoke-weary bullock
Pushed in through the open door.

'How do I know what is greatest,
How do I know what is least?
That is my Father's business,'
Said Eddi, Wilfrid's priest.

'But – three are gathered together
Listen to me and attend,
I bring good news, my brethren!'
Said Eddi of Manhood End.

And he told of the Ox of a Manger
And a Stall in Bethlehem,
And he spoke to the Ass of a Rider
That rode to Jerusalem.

They steamed and dripped in the chancel,
They listened and never stirred,
While, just as though they were Bishops,
Eddi preached them The Word.

Till the gale blew off on the marshes,
And the windows showed the day,
And the Ox and the Ass together
Wheeled and clattered away.

And when the Saxons mocked him,
Said Eddi of Manhood End,
'I dare not shut His chapel
On such as care to attend!'

Rudyard Kipling

With acknowledgements to the church of St Wilfrid
where this poem is displayed.

ST. ANDREW, DIDLING.

Didling, St Andrew

Nestling under Didling Hill and just off Bugshill Lane near Bepton is the little church of St Andrew, known as 'the Shepherds' Church'. Its isolation gives it prominence among the sheep-filled fields on the slopes of the Downs. Shadowed by an ancient yew tree, the nave and chancel come under a single span roof. The Normans replaced the earlier Saxon building but, fortunately, the Saxon tub font remains. Rendering and brickwork are evidence of eighteenth and nineteenth century restoration, while the wooden north porch and single bell turret are nineteenth century.

Early English lancet windows with plain glass give a light, airy effect and the dark stained furnishings contrast well with the whitewashed walls and ceiling. Medieval bench pews and candle lighting add to the rustic ambience of a church said to be haunted by a choirboy. His apparition has not been seen but his beautiful voice has been heard, as the church notes inform: 'Soon after World War II he was heard singing by the then Rector and congregation during a Morning Service.' Visitors, be prepared for celestial accompaniment!

DIDLING HILL

Between the sea and Midhurst town,
There lies a jewel in England's crown,
Where one can almost touch and feel,
The tranquil beauty of Didling Hill.

From high above through summer's haze,
Neat fields are seen in breathless phase;
Country sounds blended in silent hush,
A lazy air that brooks no fuss.

Near the top wild raspberries grow,
And lower down the cowslips show,
Among quaking grass and orchids took,
Flit speckled wood and chalkhill blue.

Chalk exposed reveals by-gone strife,
Fossil remains of cretaceous life,
And iron pyrites in nodular form,
Thunder-bolts left from last night's storm?

Beside the church an ancient yew,
Accidentally sawn but still it grew,
And sunken lanes behold their treat,
Of bold red campion and meadow sweet.

Here primroses carpet the woodland glade,
There dog violets are found in cooler shade,
Now a glimmering stream runs crystal clear,
Bearing sweet watercress year by year.

When next you walk upon the Down,
Between the sea and Midhurst town
Cherish the beauty that lingers still,
That little gem called Didling Hill.

With acknowledgements to the
author and the church where this
poem is displayed.

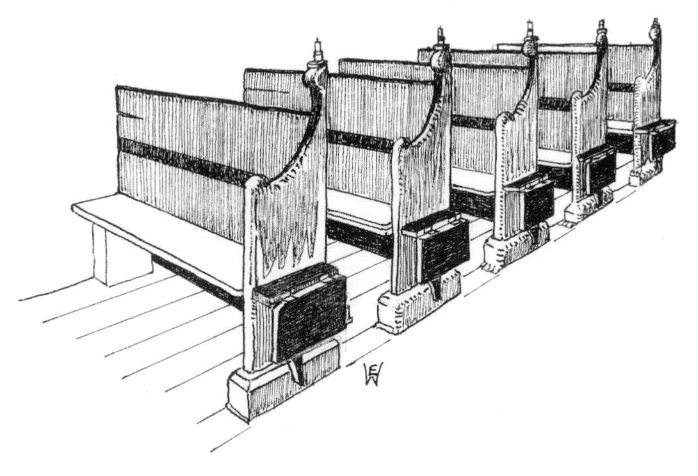

Medieval bench pews with modern additional seating

ST MARY, WEST CHILTINGTON. (SOUTH ASPECT)

The unusually long squint window

West Chiltington, St Mary

Seventeenth century Perpendicular chancel arch

The attractive village of West Chiltington has grown round the crossroads in this part of the country two miles east of Pulborough. St Mary's, with its central shingled spire and Horsham slabbed roof, is obvious along Church Lane. There is so much of interest about this building that visitors will do well to allow plenty of time for their stay. The nave and offset chancel are Norman, though reference to a church here in the *Domesday Book* indicates a Saxon original. Entrance is by the thirteenth century north porch, said to be the oldest in Sussex. One's attention is drawn immediately to the unusual Perpendicular double chancel arch, originally Norman but heightened in the seventeenth century.

At the east end of the Norman arcade a squint window (hagioscope) penetrates the Norman pillar and double chancel arch, producing a tunnel nine feet in length. As the Greek word hagioscope indicates, its purpose was to allow the holy things (bread and wine) to be seen in the act of consecration, during the Holy Communion Service, by someone standing in the south aisle. To the right of the hagioscope is the fourteenth century chantry chapel.

The octagonal thirteenth century font is typical of its period, but the *piece de resistance* among so many other interesting features are the fascinating and well-preserved thirteenth century wall paintings that were uncovered in the nineteenth century.

Thirteenth century north porch

ST. MARY, WALBERTON

The Saxon tub font on its original cushion stone

Walberton, St Mary

The church of St Mary stands on the south side of the pleasant village of Walberton. Approach to the church, not surprisingly down Church Lane, brings one to the agreeable lych-gate erected in 1920 and dedicated in December that year, along with a plaque in the church, as a memorial to the fallen in the Great War. The elegant wooden spire replicates the typical English style predominant in this part of Sussex. Prior to the thirteenth century building a Saxon church stood on the site and is mentioned in the *Domesday Book.*

One of the earliest in the county, the Saxon font is described as 'a tub or pudding-basin font'.

The stained-glass windows are exceptionally pleasing; the wide splays of the Early English lancet windows provide a natural reredos to the altar-table. The modern Woolton memorial windows at the east end of the south aisle are rich in colour and design, worthy of careful study and thought. Do not miss the west window somewhat obscured by the ringers' gallery.

NB: St Mary's twentieth century lych-gate is a fine example of 'a roofed gateway to a churchyard'. The purpose of a covered lych-gate was to provide a place for the priest to receive the coffin and offer prayers, immediately prior to processing into church for a funeral service. The name is derived from the Anglo-Saxon *lyche* – a corpse or body, and *yate* – gate.

Memorial lych-gate

ST. MARY MAGDALENE,
LYMINSTER.

Poisoning the dragon. Part of the four-panelled stained-glass vestry partition

North aisle: King-post timbers supporting the sweep of this north side roof

Lyminster, St Mary Magdalene

Turning off the A284 Lyminster Road and passing the Arundel Vineyard, the visitor is presented with an impressively picturesque view of the church with its thirteenth century tower, lych-gate and well-kept churchyard.

The church is mentioned in the *Domesday Book* and interest abounds in links with a Saxon Benedictine nunnery, a medieval nuns' church, now part of the chancel, a twelfth century font and similar-dated piscina and the Norman north aisle with its king-post roofing timbers. The little angel window and east end Mary Magdalene window are of particular interest. A fine new organ, dedicated in September 1999, has been added to the chancel. In the north aisle a scale model of Jerusalem 'as Jesus knew it' is the precise and dedicated work of a parishioner.

The legend of the Knucker Hole Dragon is graphically illustrated in the modern stained glass of the vestry partition near the font. The Knucker Hole is approximately two hundred yards away from the church along the pathway to Arundel. The story handed down is that a monster lurked in the supposedly bottomless pool, coming out to create terror and devastation in the area. Jim Pulk, a farmer's boy, courageously induced the dragon to eat an apple impregnated with poison. Jubilation attended the death of the dragon with celebrations in the Six Bells. Triumph turned to tragedy as young Jim imbibed some of the poison still on his hands; he died and was buried in the churchyard. Recently Jim's tombstone was brought into the church and placed on the wall east of the font, close to the stained glass commemorative panel.

ST. NICHOLAS, POLING.

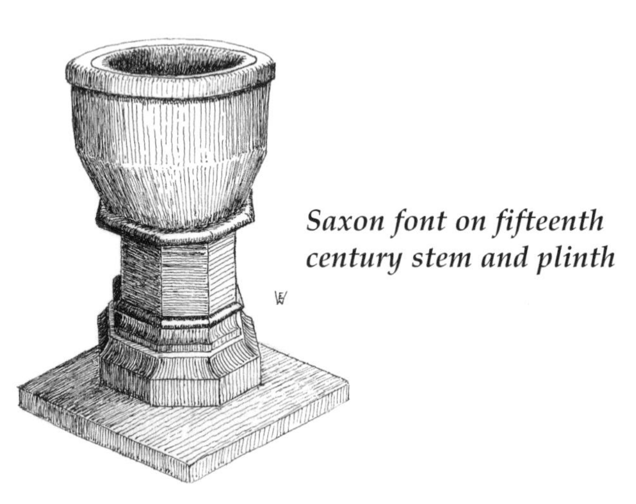

Saxon font on fifteenth century stem and plinth

Poling, St Nicholas

Turn off the A27 at Poling Corner into Poling Street, one mile beyond Angmering. The remains of the Knights Hospitallers' Priory of St John of Jerusalem are immediately to the left. Near the end of the cul-de-sac a pathway leads past manor buildings to the church, hidden at this point by yews and willows, the weathervane alone visible above the trees.

The pathway which leads to the nearby Roman villa goes through the churchyard and, suddenly, in the clearing the church of St Nicholas comes into full view. The Normans added to the original Saxon building and the heavily buttressed tower was built in the fifteenth century.

Entering by the nineteenth century south porch the visitor will see an ancient poor box fastened to the south aisle wall immediately to the right. The only ancient poor box in Sussex, it bears a restoration date of 1797, a salutary reminder of the social ministry of the Church over the centuries.

The Saxon font is supported on its fifteenth century stem and plinth, and a Saxon window survives in the north wall of the nave.

Interesting memorials, reredos murals and fifteenth century windows make for well-spent time by the visitor.

St Nicholas, patron saint of seafarers. A pleasant effigy prominent in the sanctuary

St. Mary, Barlavington

Edwin Wilkinson.

One of the tree seats in the churchyard

Barlavington, St Mary

Turn off the A29 approximately three and a half miles south of Petworth, and the hamlet will be seen nestling close to the Downs. St Mary's and Barlavington Farm are at the end of the country lane sharing the beauty of the setting. Barlavington is in the benefice of Sutton along with Burton, Coates and Bignor. St Mary's is a simple building comprising a nave, south aisle and chancel, built with local stone in the Early English period (*c*1200AD), and the pointed arches and twin lancet windows at the east end are typical of this period.

The south aisle and bell-turret were rebuilt in the nineteenth century. A very fine oak carving of the Annunciation provides a fitting focal point behind the Holy table, given in 1970 by Mrs Holland of Sutton End, a former churchwarden, and carved by Arthur Ayres, a sculptor renowned for his church work, especially the west wall figures in Wells Cathedral.

In the churchyard there is a novel adaptation of two cypress tree stumps, cut to form seats. Apparently both are well used by visitors for photo sessions.

Carved oak Annunciation

A medieval pilgrim's Virgin and Child incised on a pillar

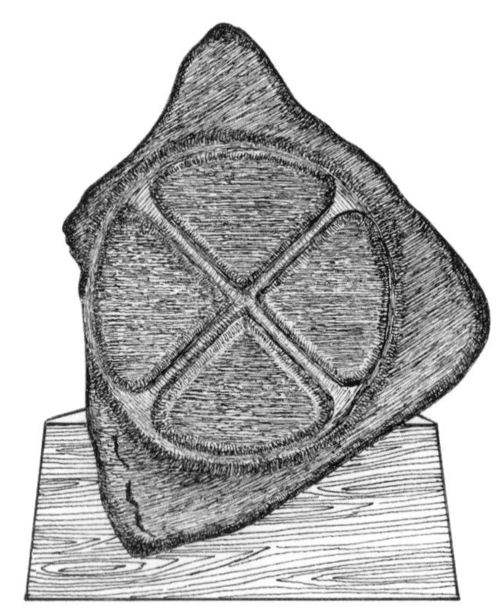

Displayed stone cross from the original Saxon church

West Wittering, St Peter and St Paul

From the main road, at the west end of the village, turn off on the beach road and then turn immediately right on the slip road which runs between the church and the primary school. The largely Norman church building replaced an earlier Saxon church destroyed by the Danes. The font, and the displayed stone cross, may well have been part of the original church building.

The saintly Richard, Bishop of Chichester (1245-1253) had close links with West Wittering church, and the remarkable broken slab in the lady chapel is engraved with the symbols of a bishop. Whether that bishop was St Richard of Chichester is not known, but the association remains intriguing. St Richard died in 1253 and his well-visited shrine remained in the cathedral at Chichester for 300 years until it was smashed, and the saint's body removed to a site unknown even to this day, during Henry VIII's upheavals.

A medieval incised outline of the Virgin and Child is among the pilgrim crossses on the eastern pillar of the thirteenth century south arcade. The now very faint original is helpfully reproduced on a separate piece of stone. Some forty votive crosses were at one time visible, indicating 'the existence in the middle ages of a shrine close by', according to the church guide.

Two notable sixteenth century Ernley family memorials in the chancel reflect the victory of the Resurrection, particular to the smaller tomb is the addition of the Lily-Crucifix, a form of symbol found only in England. Tudor misericords are to be found in the nearby stalls. The north-central position of the thirteenth century tower is unusual, the nineteenth century east end lancet windows elegantly in keeping.

It is well worth covering the Selsey peninsular to pay this church a visit, as did St Richard of old whose inspired prayer still moves us:

Thanks be to thee, my Lord Jesus Christ
For all the benefits which thou hast won for me;
For all the pains and insults which thou hast borne for me.
O most merciful Redeemer, Friend and Brother,
May I know thee more clearly, love thee more dearly,
And follow thee more nearly, day by day.
Amen.

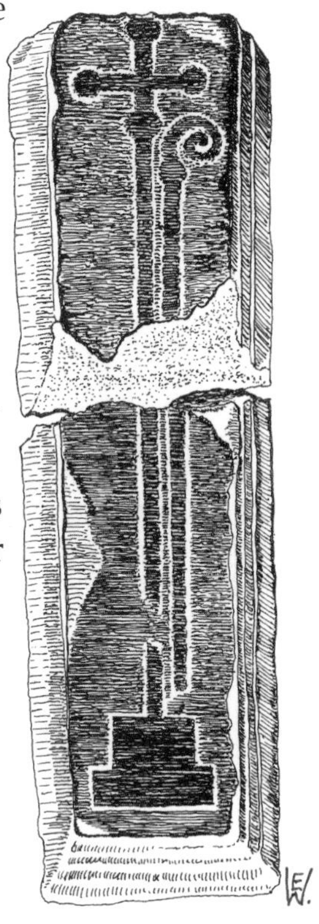

The broken slab

St. Laurence, Lurgashall.

Lurgashall, St Laurence

Four miles north of Petworth turn off the A283 on to the minor road which in one mile leads into Lurgashall. The village green, companion cottages, village pub and adjacent church nestling amid protective trees, is classical rural Sussex. As the visitor approaches the church, on the pathway through the trees, the sixteenth century lean-to addition is an immediate and unusual feature stretching the entire south side of the nave. Intended originally as a covered waiting area for worshippers, it was used for many years as the village school. More recently part of it has been made into a vestry and is the covered way into the church.

In the nave an 'Act of Parliament Clock', made and donated to the church by John Wilding in 1999, is a beautiful token of dedicated craftsmanship as also are the bracketed and adapted oil-lamp lights used throughout the nave. A colourful and imaginative millennium window by Philippa Martin depicts aspects of village activities and associations alongside St Laurence, the patron saint of the church.

Act of Parliament clock

St Laurence was treasurer and archdeacon of the Church in Rome when the Emperor Valerian demanded its 'treasures' be handed over to him. Laurence produced the sick and poor, orphans and widows, and presented them as 'the greatest treasures of the Church'. Valerian had the saint put to death in 285AD by burning on a grid-iron, consequently the grid-iron is the usual emblem of St Laurence, and is depicted on the weather-vane of the church at Lurgashall.

The un-aisled high walled nave, and herring-bone masonry in the north and south walls, confirm the Saxon origins of the church. Strikingly heavy in appearance is the cube-proportioned Sussex marble font bearing the date 1661. Apparently the first use of the font coincided with the introduction of the 1662 *Book of Common Prayer*, still the official Service Book of the Church.

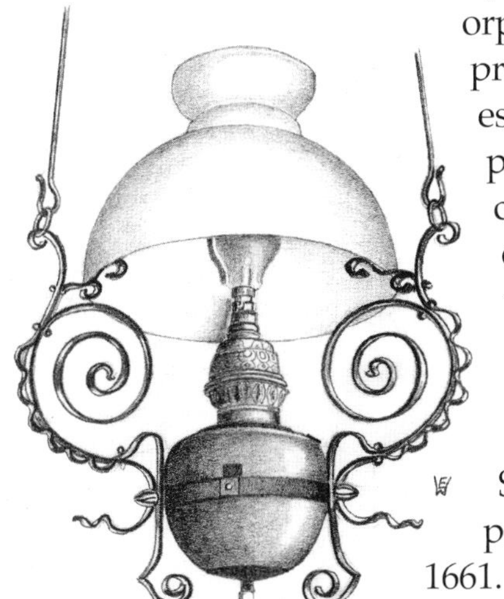

Adapted lighting in the nave

Impression of John Lee's 1961 bronze plaque

Trotton, St George

Turn off the A272 at Trotton Bridge, two miles from Midhurst. The early Norman church was rebuilt in 1300AD and provided with a thatched roof which itself was replaced approximately one hundred years later. The tower was built in 1230AD, and the relatively plain nave and chancel are contained in one over-all chamber.

Associations with the prestigious Camoys family link the church firmly in the history of the county and the nation. The Camoys memorial tomb has a central position in the line of the communion rails. Apart from the intended closeness to the altar the present effect may have been heightened by the removal of the large rood screen after the Reformation. The renowned memorial brass on top of the tomb-chest is almost life-size. Equally worthy of note is the 1310AD memorial brass to Margaret, Lady Camoys, which is reputed to be the oldest brass of a woman in the country. For preservation it is under the carpet in the nave but can be viewed with permission.

High quality fourteenth century red monochrome murals cover the west wall of the nave and are worthy of careful study. On the left carnal man is depicted disobeying the Commandments by partaking in the Seven Deadly Sins. To the right the spiritually inclined man is shown fulfilling the Seven Works of Mercy.

Brass to Thomas, Lord Camoys, 1419, and wife

Acknowledgements to Yale University Press

In the porch is a striking St George plaque in bronze metal-work by John Lee, 1961, a very effective twentieth century contribution.

The plain appearance of the church is deceptive. Little by little fascinating treasures of history yield to the enquiring mind.

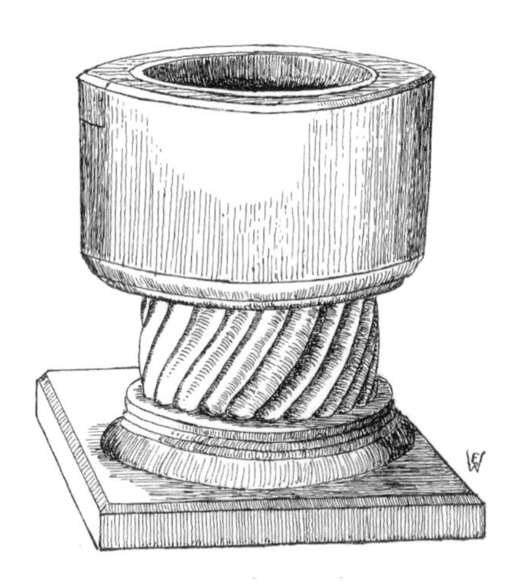

Saxon font

North Mundham, St Stephen

One mile south of Chichester the church is situated on the south edge of North Mundham village. Dedicated to St Stephen, it is a large, well-maintained parish church of thirteenth century origin, effectively restored in the nineteenth century when the chancel and vestry were added.

The nineteenth century stained glass and wrought iron chancel screen add distinctive character and interest to the church. The font, which measures 39in across, is cut from a single block of Sussex marble and is one of the largest in Sussex. It may well have been made and provided for the original local church, though an earlier date is possible, in which case the font pre-dates the parish church it has served for eight centuries. A beautifully carved nineteenth century font cover resides in the west gallery, hopefully awaiting re-housing on the hooks and pulleys to fulfil its intended use.

There are a number of fascinating memorials to engage the visitor, but that to John Bigs presents the discomforting logic, 'As I was so are ye, as I am so shall ye be!'

Nineteenth century font cover

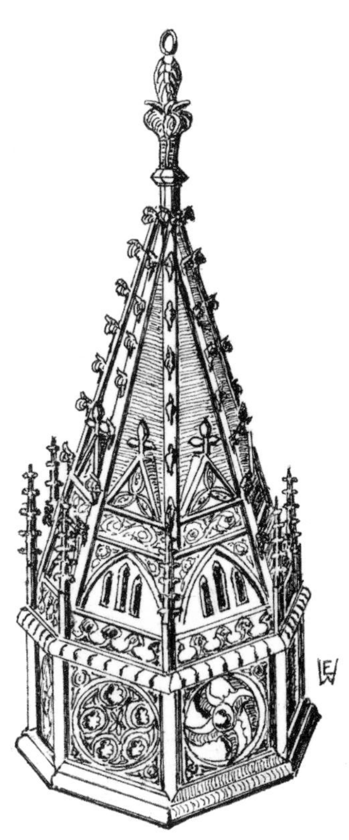

ST. PETER AD VINCULA,
WISBOROUGH GREEN.

Wisborough Green, St Peter ad Vincula

Fifteenth century north porch

Two miles beyond Billingshurst on the A272 the church is prominent on the higher ground at the eastern end of the village. The dedication to St Peter ad Vincula (St Peter in Chains – see the *Acts of the Apostles* ch12 v6) is rare. Including this there are only ten such dedications in England.

Herringbone masonry in the west wall indicates an Anglo-Saxon, eleventh century beginning to the church. The thirteenth century tower is an extension of the eleventh century west wall, the additional fourteenth century shingle spire making an outstanding landmark. A relatively small west door has been supplemented by two fifteenth century porches leading into the nave from the north and south. The wooden north porch is the present entrance while the formerly impressive south porch is disused.

Two works of art in the nave are engaging, namely, a medieval mural on the chancel arch in which the artist has portrayed, unusually, Jesus and the two thieves crucified together on a common wooden scaffold. On the north wall is the beautiful Wisborough Tapestry made by the villagers and bearing the date 1977. Aspects of village life or history are depicted in sixty-five roundels in three conjoined panels, bordered with forty vignettes illustrating local flora and fauna. Designed with imagination and worked with immense dedication and skill, the tapestry is a superb piece of art.

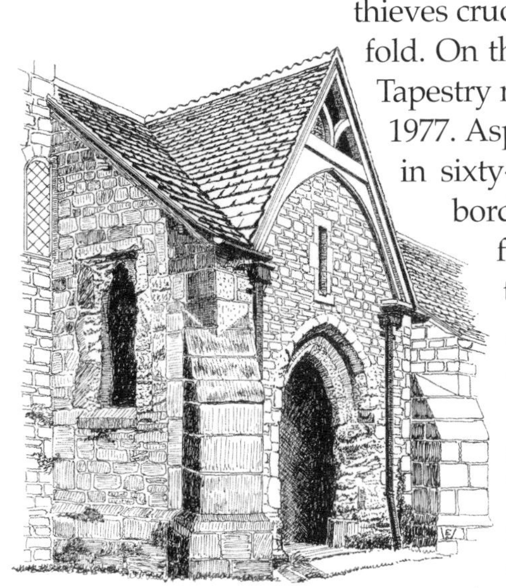

Disused south porth

A stone altar against the east wall of the sanctuary replaced a wooden Communion Table in 1937, reflecting a pre-Reformation tradition. The thirteenth century lancet windows and Victorian stained glass, make an effective and attractive reredos.

ST. MARY, BILLINGSHURST.

Billingshurst, St Mary

Situated near the centre of the town, the church is a prominent feature over the junction of the A272 with the A29, the old Roman Stane Street.

The fifteenth century 120ft broach spire was added to the thirteenth century tower, its additional weight making necessary the heavy clasp buttressing of the tower.

Eight bells are housed in the tower, and the clock on its west side has a mechanism which is a half-size replica of the works in Westminster's famous Big Ben. Always advisable to look upwards in any church, it is especially desirable here. The nave has an impressive fifteenth century wagon-vault with square panels and oak bosses all of different design. Wagon-wheel chandeliers add an interesting and highly individualistic feature in the nave. Also in the nave, but at floor level close to the chancel arch, is a memorial brass to Thomas and Elizabeth Bartlett of Okehurst, bearing the date 1499. The blocked window high in the west wall of the nave was probably a 'watching window' used by the ringers in the bell-chamber.

The stained-glass windows, nineteenth century throughout, are admirable in their beauty of design and colour, especially those in the spiritually warm Lady Chapel, which induces devotion even in the casual visitor.

Enterprisingly, the Children's Corner was displaying framed and named portraits of all the young church members bearing the caption to each – 'I am precious to God'. In the centre of the display a framed mirror bore the caption 'You are precious to God!' A delightfully arresting application.

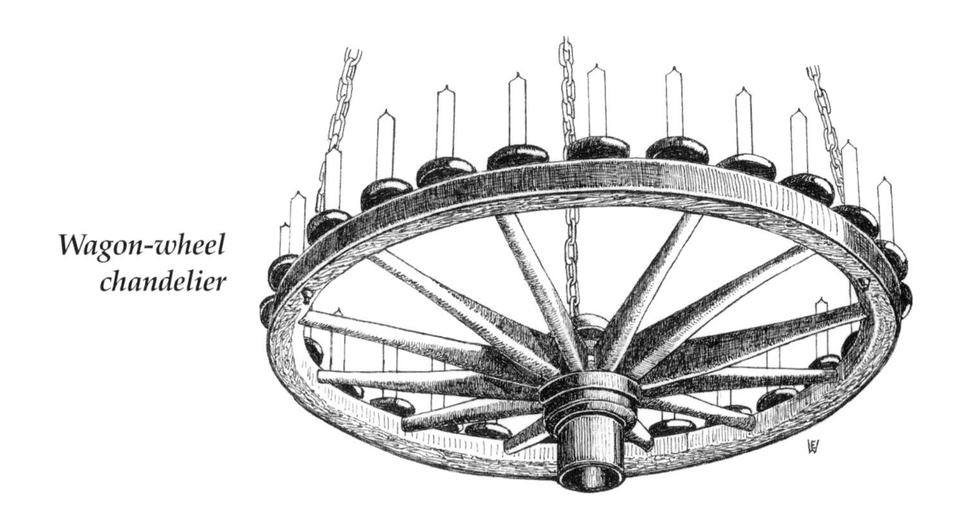

Wagon-wheel chandelier

ST JOHN BAPTIST, SUTTON.

Sutton, St John the Baptist

Turn off the A29 Pulborough to Arundel road and follow the line of the Downs through West Burton and Bignor to Sutton. The church stands at the northern edge of the picturesque village, its clean architecture an impressive feature in warm Pulborough stone. Though the nave is twelfth century, herringbone masonry in the north wall suggests an even earlier building.

The well-buttressed fourteenth century tower is topped with a shingled 'Sussex cap'. Circular twelfth century columns support the south arcade with the delightful thirteenth century font in juxtaposition. In the chancel south wall are the classic fourteenth century sedilia (clergy seats), and trefoiled piscina where the Communion vessels were washed. The open wooden Communion Table is effective in its symbolic simplicity, and is backed by a Lamb of God carving in the central panel of the reredos. The latticed iron work, with metal roses on the intersections, adds unusual and pleasant character to the already sturdy oak communion rails.

The visitor to this impressive church may like to ponder whether the moulded arch at the south east corner of the exterior wall (clearly featured in the drawing) is all that remains of a twelfth century altar-tomb, a rather rare feature.

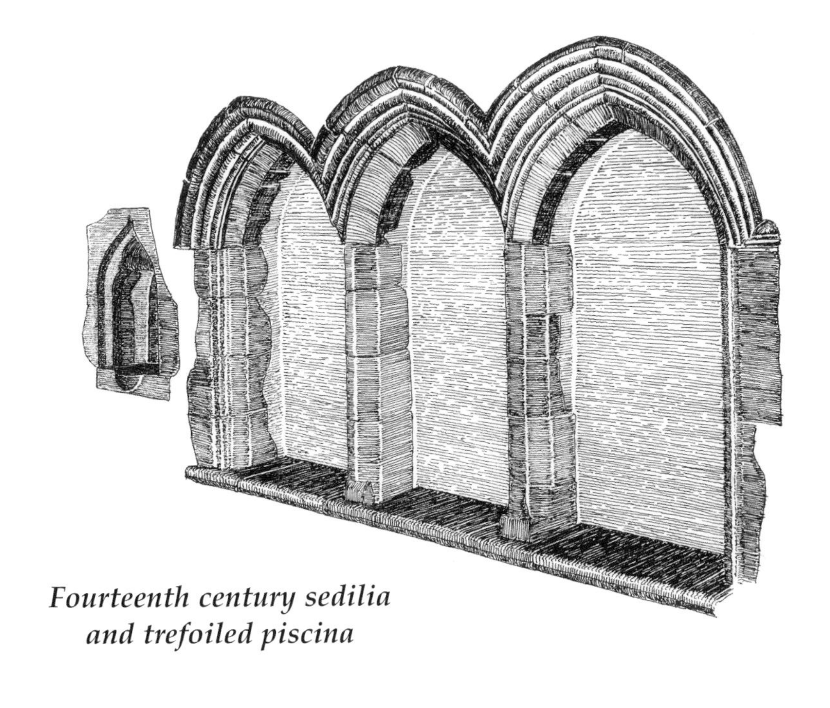

Fourteenth century sedilia and trefoiled piscina

ST. JAMES, HEYSHOTT.

Design of east window

Design of south chancel window

Heyshott, St James

Two miles south of Midhurst off the A286, the church of St James stands on the northern edge of Heyshott village, in luscious countryside near the Downs.

A thirteenth century building replaced an earlier church, in its turn to be largely replaced by the nineteenth century building as it is today. The stained-glass of the east window is modern with a less usual uniform design in Decorated style depicting the cross, and the Greek abbreviation of the name Jesus – IHC. This monogram is one of the earliest symbols used by Christians. Its use here, as with the cross, has a strong association with the celebration of the Eucharist. The modern glass uniform leaf design of the south window in the chancel is also unusual and may be indicative of creation's bounty, the hopeful seeds of resurrection and life, spiritual life and fruitfulness. The church guide suggests that the tub-shaped original part of the font was used in the pre-thirteenth century church, a plausible idea.

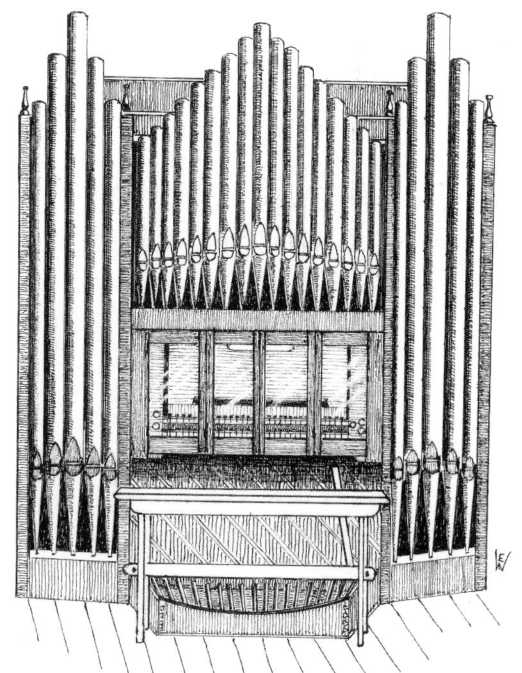

Tracker organ

Prominent at the west end is a delightful twin console Tracker organ which was built in 1931 for Hildersham School in Broadstairs. When the school closed in 1971 the then organist, Derek Gaye, bought the instrument and presented it to the church in memory of his mother.

Students of social history will find interest in the link with Richard Cobden (1805-1865), leader of the Anti-Corn Law League, who attended the church; a plaque marks his place in the front pew.

Notably one of the three bells in the shingle steeple is fourteenth century, the others are seventeenth century.

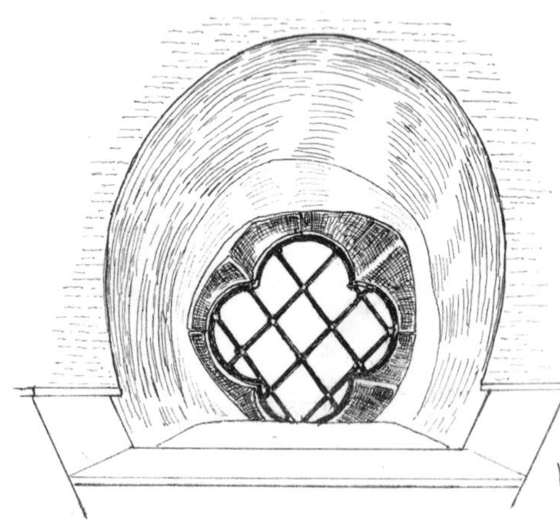

Remarkably low window in the shallow south aisle wall

Yapton, St Mary the Virgin

The village of Yapton lies a mile and a half due north of Middleton-on-Sea, with the parish church of St Mary the Virgin on its northern edge. The church is a flint building of Saxon origin endowed with many irregular angles, but it is an architectural gem not to be missed.

The heavily buttressed twelfth century tower has a tilt of eleven degrees and its shingled nineteenth century Sussex cap had to be shaped to accommodate the angles.

The limestone Saxon font, with its chevrons representing the Water of Life, and crosses signifying the Sword of the Spirit, has been in use within the building throughout its thousand-year existence.

Twelfth-thirteenth century south arcade

Pilgrims have at some time carved votive crosses on the interior stonework, mainly on the hexagonal pillars of the south arcade, where there is also a three inch diameter consecration cross roughly incised in the stone.

The windows are interesting and varied, rewarding careful attention following the details as set out in the helpful guide book. A strong contrast in effectiveness is obvious between the seventeenth century dormer windows and the remarkable low round windows in the south aisle wall. The east end Collins memorial window by N J H Westlake (1902) is rich in colour and design.

Among many interesting memorials is that to Stephen Roe whose Charity Fund was set up in 1766; some parishioners still benefit from the fund. Part of the memorial inscription reads:

By bounty taught and fed.
Orphans and Widows more and more,
And children yet unborn shall pour
Their blessings on him dead.

If 'thankfulness' characterizes the Stephen Roe memorial, 'thoughtfulness' is prompted by the John Green gravestone (1754) alongside the west porch entrance:

All you that pass this way along,
Think you how sudden I was gone.
God doth not always warning give
Therefore be careful how you live.

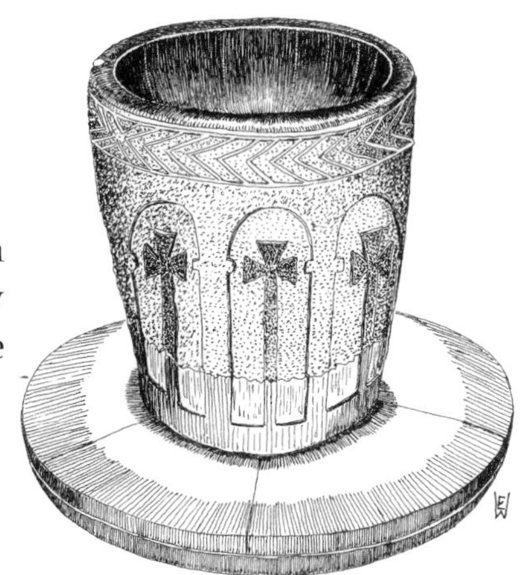

Saxon limestone font

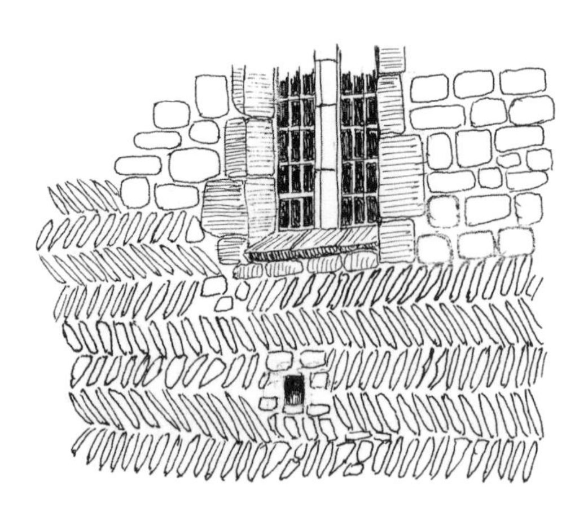

Saxon herringbone work in the west wall. Note the small leper window

Elsted, St Paul

Four miles west of Midhurst on the road to Harting, the hamlet of Elsted has gradually arisen on the south side of the Saxon church of St Paul. A surprising building in appearance, it is mentioned in the *Domesday Book*.

Large sections of Saxon herringbone walling, especially in the west wall exterior, provide an excellent example of this type of masonry, said to be the finest in the county. High in the west wall is the unusual hexagonal window, unashamedly twentieth century, while low in the same wall is the leper window through which a leper could observe the celebration of the Mass but isolated from the congregation.

Twentieth century hexagon window and leper squint in the west wall

A Norman chancel was replaced by the larger Early English chancel extant today.

The south porch date-stone of 1662 shows its addition coincided with the introduction of *The Book of Common Prayer,* still authorised for use in the Church of England.

From 1850 St Paul's fell upon hard times. It was neglected when a new church opened at nearby Treyford in 1893, and suffered severe damage to the nave roof caused by a falling tree. Apart from the chancel, the church became virtually derelict, but its fortunes took a dramatic turn from 1947 with the demolition of Treyford church and the appointment of an enthusiastic parish priest for St Paul's, the Reverend F E Parkhouse. Under his general directive the church building was restored and re-dedicated in 1951 by Bishop George Bell of Chichester. The medieval bell was re-cast in 1973 and housed in its unusual, but practical, position between the nave and chancel roofs. The bell is rung from alongside the rector's stall in the chancel.

Re-cast medieval bell in its roof housing

This is a church full of surprises well worth seeking.

ST. MARY THE VIRGIN, BURPHAM.

Burpham, St Mary the Virgin

Turn off the A27 at Arundel railway station and follow the cul-de-sac road along the Arun valley through Wepham to Burpham. The impressive fourteenth century tower of St Mary's is soon in view between the buildings in the village.

To visitors entering the basically Norman church with its excellent Victorian renovations, the most striking feature is the vaulted ceiling of the chancel with the beautiful proportions and aesthetic line.

At the east end of the chancel the wide splays of the lancet windows, renovated in the fourteenth century, suggest a link with the original Norman building.

The nineteenth and twentieth century stained glass throughout the building is richly coloured. The east end panels show St Peter and St Paul on either side of the main detail that depicts Christ's birth and crucifixion. The modern north aisle memorial window, skilfully designed on the theme of eagle wings, and bearing the RAF Insignia, is of particular interest.

Nineteenth century lectern

As well as the delights of the church, vistas of the valley and Arundel are there for the visitor to enjoy.

Early English ribbed-vaulted chancel

St. Margaret,

R.A.F. Insignia on a memorial to Fl. Officer William Rodney Stewart King.

'Through adversity to the stars'

Coat of Arms on a memorial to Lt Commander Gerald Hildred Elsdale Molson, RN, a gunnery officer on HMS Rawalpindi sunk by the Scharnhorst and Gneisenau, 23.11.39

Vine and angel carvings on the nave arcades

Angmering, St Margaret

The imposing sixteenth century tower survives from an earlier church of Norman origin replaced by the present building in 1853 through the generous gift of William Gratwicke. In dimensions the building is as broad as it is long. The Victorian preference for congregational participation is reflected in the light openness created by the structure. A place of worship well used and cared for.

The chancel arch and the archway to the south porch are part of the earlier building. Interestingly, Lottie Gray Horton's memorial window is said to be 200-years-old. Is it also a survivor from the earlier building?

The old church hall (the vestry hall), in the immediate approach to the church, was restored in 1994, and fulfils the stated aim 'to provide a place of warmth and rest for passers-by'. Visitors find welcome refresments available.

ST. PETER, COWFOLD.

Fourteenth century stained-glass sections, chancel north side windows

Cowfold, St Peter

The church stands on the crossroads of the A272 and A281 between the main residential areas of the large village. The churchyard has been designated a nature conservation area, accordingly receiving minimum mowing, its north side bounded by the picturesque Margaret Cottages.

A thirteenth century chancel, fifteenth century nave and tower, and additional sixteenth century south aisle, blend into a unity of strength and solidarity, roofed over-all with Horsham slate. Complementary Horsham stone slabs are used on the approach to the impressive fifteenth century carved oak north porch.

The famous brass memorial to Thomas Nelond, 1429, Prior of St Pancras, Lewes, is of great value and interest. The large brass – 10ft 2in in length and 4ft 8in wide – in the main aisle, is now covered for protection, but postcard illustrations and detailed information about the brass are available for the visitor.

Stained glass, largely Victorian, is excellent all round the church, but especially the Kempe window in the south aisle depicting the Adoration of the Shepherds.The north side lancet windows in the chancel contain a small but rare thirteenth-fourteenth century stained glass depiction of the Crucifixion. St Mary, St John and a Jewish official are shown near the cross. Other symbols in the composition include a fishing boat and nets, vine leaves and cowslips. The ascription which was placed at the head of the cross – Jesus of Nazareth, the King of the Jews – is represented by the first letters of the Latin *'Iesus Nazarenus Rex Ludaeorum'*.

These items, and more, will stimulate the interested visitor.

The Margaret Cottages, St Peter's Churchyard, Cowfold.

Off-set nineteenth century bell-turret

Eastergate, St George

Modern sculpture of the church's patron saint

Turn off the Littlehampton Road at the edge of the village and approach the church through Manor Farm with its notable seventeenth century brick and timber barn. The church of St George is an uncomplicated building – with no buttresses. The herringbone ribbing in the exterior south wall of the chancel and the small window in the chancel north wall, are evidence of the church's Saxon origins. The Norman modifications and Victorian restoration have contributed largely to the church's present appearance.

The off-set nineteenth century bell-turret houses one bell inscribed in memory of John Boniface Jnr, churchwarden, and dated 1737.

Two modern works – a tapestry, History of Eastergate, and a wood carving of the church's patron saint, contribute to the variety of interest in this well-used church.

THE OLD BARN (A.D 1600) AT MANOR FARM,

STORRINGTON, ST. MARY.

Brass plate memorial to Henry Wilsha

Storrington, St Mary

The parish church of St Mary at Storrington is sited on the impressive sandstone escarpment on the southern edge of the village. Its origin is Norman, and it is mentioned in the *Domesday Book*; there are many notable features contributed through the centuries.

The Anvil Window

The substantial tower supported a tall fine spire until it was struck by lightning in 1731. Private galleries erected in the eighteenth century did not survive the major restoration of 1873 when open seating was introduced throughout the church in accord with the mood of the time. At the time of this restoration a beautifully crafted Caen-stone reredos was added behind the altar, the three sections depicting The Changing of Water into Wine, The Ascension of Jesus, The Feeding of the Five Thousand.

The stained glass windows are outstanding, especially the Tabitha window in the south aisle, and the round Anvil window in the tower. Among other fine memorials the sixteenth century brass in memory of the former rector Henry Wilsha, 1551-1591, is rare. Modern seasonal altar-covers are striking for their beauty of design and skilled needlework. A store of delights await the interested visitor to this well kept church.

NB: The round Anvil Window in the tower depicts St Dunstan, Archbishop of Canterbury and patron saint of blacksmiths, the furnace, anvil, and tools of the forge, along with the Canterbury coat of arms. The window is a memorial to Samuel Huffer – verger, clerk and blacksmith. The inscriptions round the circumference read: 'In the handywork of their craft is their prayer'. 'Praise God for Samuel Huffer, Verger of this church who departed this life March 2, 1931'. 'Grant him, O Lord, eternal rest'.

St Dunstan (908-988) became a Benedictine monk, for a time living as a hermit, tradition making him a painter, magician and metalworker. He was appointed Abbot of Glastonbury, Bishop of Worcester and Bishop of London before becoming Archbishop of Canterbury in 960AD.

St. John the Baptist, Kirdford.

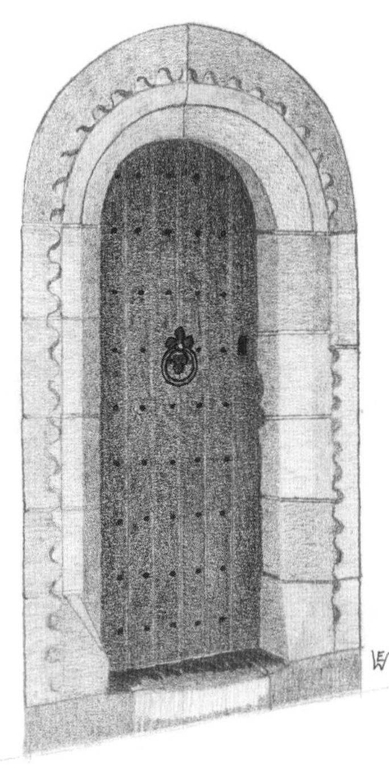

Fifteenth century studded door leading to the sacristy

Kirdford, St John the Baptist

Set in the glorious Wealden countryside, approximately five miles west of Billingshurst, St John the Baptist church stands on the southern edge of pleasant Kirdford.

The earlier entrance to the twelfth century church is blocked but can be seen with its heavy mouldings in the south wall along with herringbone masonry from the original building. Entrance is now through the little porch and impressive west tower which houses a ringers gallery and six bells. The gallery is accessed by the stone stairs round a central column, *ie* a newel stair. In the ground area of the tower look for four carved corbels representing the heads of a bull, a lion, and two human masks.

In the nave a thirteenth century three-bay arcade replaced the original north wall when the north aisle was added. An unusual and beautiful fourteenth century reticulated window makes an effective focal point at the east end of the north aisle.

The squint windows on either side of the chancel arch are unusual for their large size either in their original form when the chancel was rebuilt in the fifteenth century, or enlarged some time later.

In the chancel a heavily studded fifteenth century door has its original oak-cased lock and ring handle and leads to the small and remarkably designed sacristy, all part of the fifteenth century enlargement of the chancel.

Not unusually, the stained glass throughout the church is nineteenth century. The octagonal Sussex marble font dated 1620 was given in memory of two churchwardens, Henry Strudwick and Richard Penfold.

If the visitor is able to take advantage of the seating near the rhododendrons in the large churchyard, it will add pleasure to an already stimulating visit.

Enlarged squint (south chancel)

ST. GEORGE, WEST GRINSTE

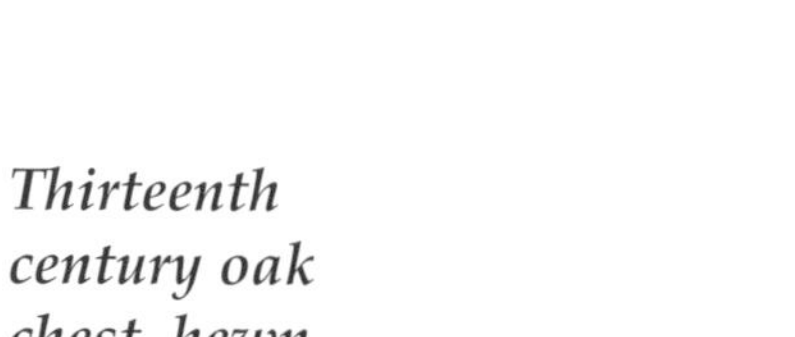

Thirteenth century oak chest, hewn from a solid piece of wood

West Grinstead, St George

Close to where the A272 meets the A24 from the east, join the minor road then turn into the lane signed 'Parish Church' and follow it past the Glebe House and farm to the church.

The extremely wide apron of the broach spire is a striking feature, as is the Horsham stone roofing of the entire church including the notable fifteenth century north porch. Heavy buttressing and rendering make unusually sharp lines to the south aspect. Before entering the church look for the large section of herringbone zigzag masonry to the right of the porch.

Conspicuous on entering are the names of farms in the parish written on the backs of the nave pews, a reminder of the discontinued custom of pew rents. In this case, apparently, males from the farms would sit in the named areas while the females sat in the pews at the rear of the nave.

A twelfth century font, elegant twentieth century rood screen, and beautifully carved and gilded reredos panels, depicting the Annunciation, add significantly to the church's character. The large Rysbrack memorial, with figures in Roman style, may seem somewhat out of character, but what superb carvings in tribute to the Powlett family. Be careful not to leave before finding the thirteenth century chest carved from a solid piece of oak and once used for church records.

Names of parish farms on pews

ST. GILES, COLDWALTHAM.

Coldwaltham, St Giles

Two miles south of Pulborough, St Giles' Church is situated on the opposite side of the A29 to the hamlet of Coldwaltham which it serves, and is close to the old Roman Road of Stane Street.

An eleventh century gravestone, a Saxon font, and the ancient yew tree, suggest collective evidence for the existence of a Saxon church on this site. As it stands today the building is mainly Norman, apart from the eighteenth century shingle cap on the tower, and the north aisle, vestry and organ chamber added a little later by the Victorians.

The nineteenth century stained glass throughout the church is impressive, as is the marble reredos with its angels and central symbol of the victorious Lamb of God (Jesus) under the flowing Easter banner.

The chapel in the north aisle was designed by the Reverend Roger Hodgson, vicar of the parish from 1982 to 1992. Most unusually the chapel is dedicated to Holy Wisdom, presumably with the classic passage of *Proverbs 8* in mind where 'Wisdom' is personified as being with God in the beginning of creation, and all who find wisdom find life in God.

Recently established as being 3,000 years old, the famous yew tree in the north-west corner of the churchyard is listed among the twelve oldest yews in the country. To mark the turn of the millennium sapling yews, from such trees as this and at Stedham, were blessed by the Bishop of Chichester in a Cathedral service. On request these were then distributed to parishes and establishments in the Diocese of Chichester.

Ancient yew

The Yew Tree Song

Written especially for the service at which yew tree saplings were blessed in Chichester Cathedral to mark the millennium.

Long, long ago through the mists of time
There grew the yew, sacred tree sublime.
Symbol of life and eternity,
Protector, guardian, sanctuary.
Down through the ages its strength did grow
By humble grave stones the mighty bow,
A holy marker, the Easter palm,
A deadly poison, a curing balm.
Standing alone or in stately row,
In quiet churchyards those yews still grow,
Keeping their watch by the wicket gate,
Immortal markers of God's estate.
Patient, enduring, they self renew,
Where once stood one, now grow many a yew,
Their timeless beauty for years to come,
Strength for the new millennium.
So, as we gather to plant our tree,
A branch of faith for eternity,
Hope for the future when we are gone,
The living proof that our love will live on.

ST. MARY, CLYMPING.

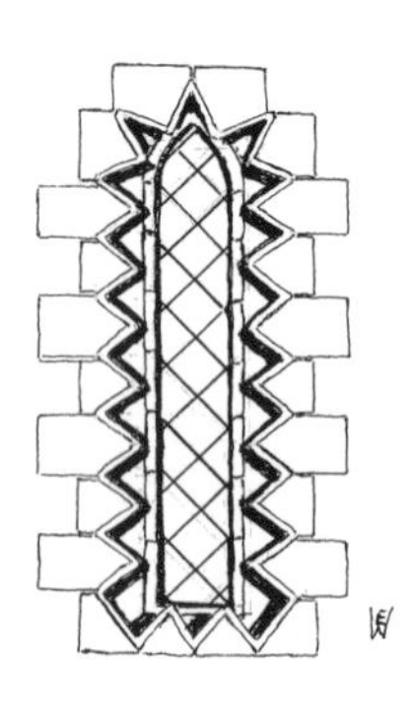

Norman moulding round the tower windows

Clymping, St Mary

Opposite Littlehampton, across the River Arun, St Mary at Clymping is approached on the Ford-Arundel road. The Norman tower immediately presents an impressive and dominant feature. Distinctive heavy moulding in zigzag and dog tooth design, from the Norman period, frame the door in the west side of the tower. The unusual zigzag moulding enwrapping the tower windows is believed to be unique in the country.

Prime mover in building this large church, virtually as it stands today, was the Reverend John de Clymping, later to become Bishop of Chichester; indeed the left hand east window in the chancel is dedicated to his memory.

The interior is beautifully spacious with wide arches, lancet windows, and fourteenth century pulpit strategically placed in its present position by the Victorians in the process of extensive restoration work. Heywood Hardy's commendable paintings, given to the church prior to his death in 1932, adorn the walls of the north transept. They depict scenes from the Birth, Death, and Resurrection of Jesus resulting in the Lady Chapel becoming known as the Chapel of Jesus.

Within the chapel is a small oak panel, presumably placed there in 1633 by the then vicar, the Reverend John White, exhorting in scriptural terms 'Walk in love' and 'Watch and pray' (*Ephesians 5* v2, and *Matthew 26* v41). Particularly relevant in the troubles of the Civil War, but timeless in their application.

The attractive church guide offers much information and reminds the reader that the church's architectural unity has brought the well-deserved appellation 'Clymping for perfection'.

A touch of Easter in the south aisle

COCKING PARISH CHURCH

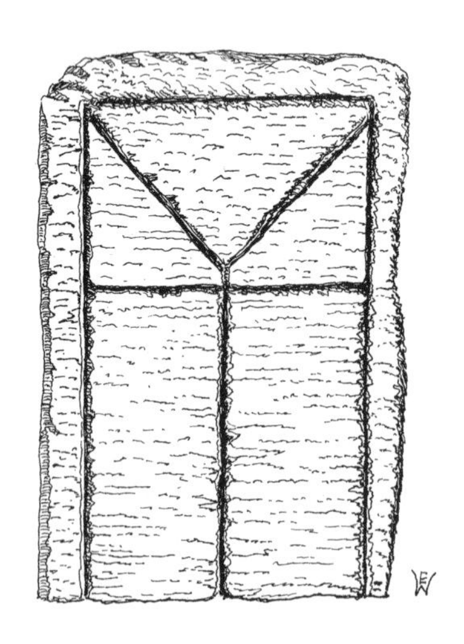

Partial Saxon grave-slab

Cocking Church (no dedication)

The church is just off the High Street on the Midhurst to Chichester main road. A short walk from the Manor Farm parking space, alongside the church, takes the visitor past the large Norman tower, now completely rendered, to the south porch entrance. Inside the Norman chancel arch is both obvious and impressive. Less obvious is the early thirteenth century mural in the splay of the south wall Norman window. An angel is depicted appearing to the Bethlehem shepherds, at the time of the Nativity. The artist brings a touch of realism to his illustration in showing the shepherd's dog barking at the angel.

Apart from the base and pedestal the font is Saxon; imagine 1,300 years of baptisms in the same font, in virtually the same place, in the same church!

A partial Saxon grave-slab was discovered during the renovations of 1865 and is mounted in the north wall of the sanctuary alongside the thirteenth century Easter Sepulchre. The slab is roughly incised with a border enclosing a V-shape atop a T (see the drawing). Without the other section of the slab the intended symbolism remains a matter for conjecture.

Plain windows prevail throughout the church except for the nineteenth century stained glass window in the chancel south wall, depicting St Richard of Chichester. The well preserved twelfth century piscina, used for washing the communion vessels, is a gem of its type.

There is much more to interest and reward the visitor to this ancient church.

Twelfth century piscina

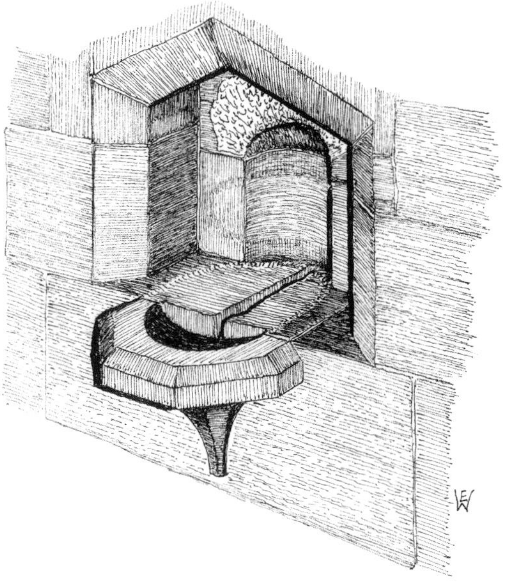

ST. ANDREW, FORD.

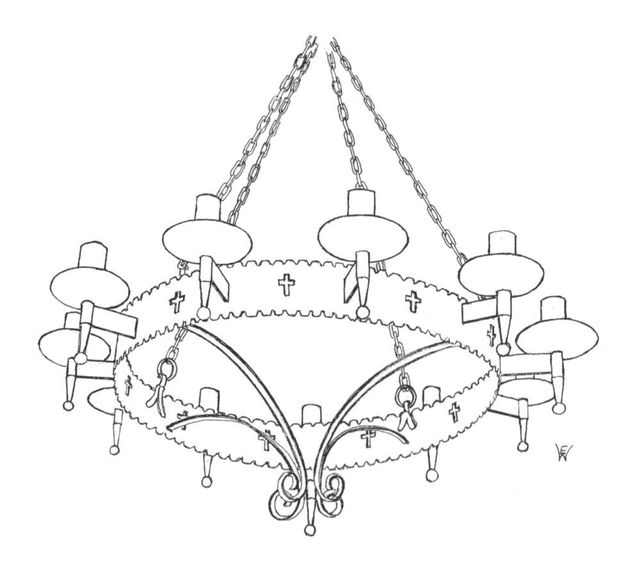

Crafted metalwork chandelier

Ford, St Andrew

Approximately one and a half miles south of Arundel on the Clymping road, this ancient little sanctuary stands on the old droving route for Chichester markets. The white-painted bell turret and seventeenth century dutch-gabled porch are obvious and attractive features from the approach.

The church was comprehensively restored in 1999, but the tenth and eleventh century features of the interior have been retained. The north and west walls of the nave are Saxon, the remainder of the building Norman. Faded thirteenth century murals are evident over the chancel arch and on the south wall of the nave.

The skilfully crafted metalwork chandeliers are very impressive, and the lighting arrangements on some of the pews pleasantly effective. The visitor may be surprised at the hard gloss black paint applied to the nineteenth century pews. This little church presents a delightful microcosm of architectural and historical interest.

Choir stall and lighting

ST. MARY THE VIRGIN, ALDINGBOURNE

The unusual Bishop's Chair, of Roman Catholic origin

Aldingbourne, St Mary the Virgin

Turn off the Nyton minor road to the White Horse Corner, then go past the hamlet to the church which stands in the wide well-kept churchyard, graced by Lebanon cedars and yew trees.

Victorian restoration is immediately evident in the rendered south wall and distinctive tower, both embattled. The church is mentioned in the *Domesday Book* and is mainly Norman, though historically there are Saxon links.

The industrious Victorians completely renovated the building in the mid-nineteenth century. There is much of interest here including a Saxon font, a double sedilia and piscina, both thirteenth century, and the ribbed vaulting in the St George's Chapel behind which is a hidden priest's room now inaccessible.

Studded ribbed vaulting in the St George Chapel (St George in the upper niche)

ST. MARY & ST. GABRIEL, HARTING.

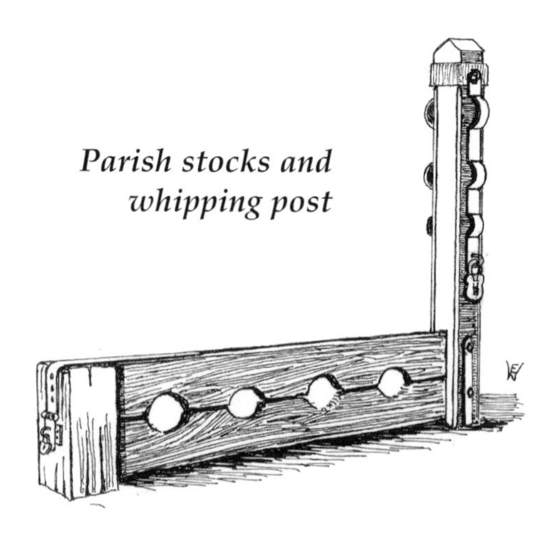

Parish stocks and whipping post

South Harting, St Mary and St Gabriel

The central tower of the church, with its broach spire, is an outstanding landmark in the attractive village of South Harting.

The church is dedicated to St Mary and St Gabriel and is the only church with that dedication in the county of Sussex. It honours the angel Gabriel's announcement to the Virgin Mary foretelling her conception and due birth of the child Jesus.

The church roofs sustained extensive damage as a result of a fire in 1576 but the restoration brought about the splendid Elizabethan rafters in the nave, north and south transepts, and especially the chancel. During the restoration opportunity was taken to lower the roofs; the former pitch lines can still be seen on the tower (see the drawing).

The *raison d'etre* of the church's purpose is well expressed by the text, from *Psalm 103,* which adorns the thirteenth century chancel arch, 'Bless the Lord, 0 my soul, and forget not all his benefits'.

A most impressive memorial is to be found in the south transept providing another Elizabethan link through John Cowper who died in 1586. The figures, probably placed there in the seventeenth century, represent John Cowper, his wife and father. The accompanying memorial tablets cover 200 years of the Cowper, Coles families. There are other notable memorials and furnishings.

The beautiful stained glass windows are mainly nineteenth century with the exception of some fourteenth century glass in the north window.

The visitor's time will be well spent here and, on leaving, the parish stocks and whipping post, just outside the churchyard gate, will provide a glimpse of social history.

Seventeenth century memorial figures

Bosham Church named and represented on the Bayeux Tapestry (1067-70)

(reproduced by permission of the vicar)

Bosham, Holy Trinity

Steeped in history, Bosham, at the head of the Bosham Channel in Chichester Harbour, is a must for would-be visitors who will find Holy Trinity church truly impressive. The Saxon tower, with its oft-renovated seventeenth century shingled spire, provides a notable and attractive coastal landmark.

Archeological discoveries establish beyond doubt a communal Roman presence as early as the first century AD. In due course Saxon builders utilised materials from a Roman basilica to erect a church on the site. The same building was renovated and extended by the Normans more or less to the proportions seen today.

King Canute's daughter is buried in the nave; King Harold, of Battle of Hastings fame, prayed in the church, as depicted on the famous Bayeux Tapestry. The church is mentioned in the *Domesday Book*.

There is much to provide architectural interest: round Saxon windows renovated by the Normans; the superb Saxon horseshoe-shaped chancel arch; a partly above ground crypt; old carved corbels; the Norman font; Flemish stained glass in the roundel windows and more besides. Holy Trinity's architectural features and historical associations are fascinating indeed.

The parish chest (illustrated) is made of thick Sussex oak and is close to being 800 years old. For centuries it was housed in the vestry and held the official documents, communion vessels and registers. It is now to be seen in the chancel.

Thirteenth century parish chest

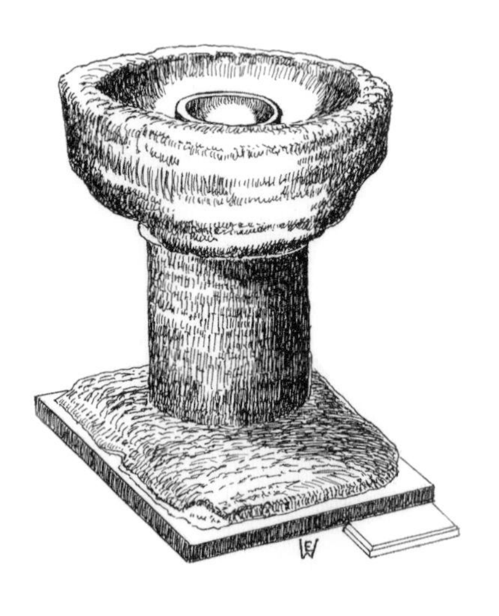

Thirteenth century font

Findon, St John the Baptist

Follow the A24 northward along the Findon Valley from Worthing and Cissbury Ring appears on the right. Within a mile turn left off the dual carriageway past Findon Place. The flint-walled church with its shingled broach-spire appears immediately on the approach. In spring snowdrops abound in the churchyard and immediate surrounds.

Inside, the nineteenth century windows immediately impress, as do the modern oak-coloured pews and tiled floor. At the point of entry the visitor is standing where the original Saxon church stood, now the north aisle, the old font at its west end may be standing where a Saxon font once stood. When the Normans arrived they added what is now the main aisle and chancel, joining the two sections by means of the arcade, making the area of the church much as it is today. The tower, along with the north and south chapels were added in the fifteenth century.

Gilbert Scott's extensive nineteenth century restoration retained the rare thirteenth century oak screen in the north aisle. Beautiful additions during the restoration were William Morris's tiled panels behind the altar-table. The ensemble of musician angels, depicted in delicate indigo, blue and gold against a leafy orchard background, are almost ethereal. Angels are a popular theme in chancels, but these are very special.

Ninteenth century tile-work – an angel ensemble

STEDHAM, ST. JAMES.

Pre-Saxon
stone coffin

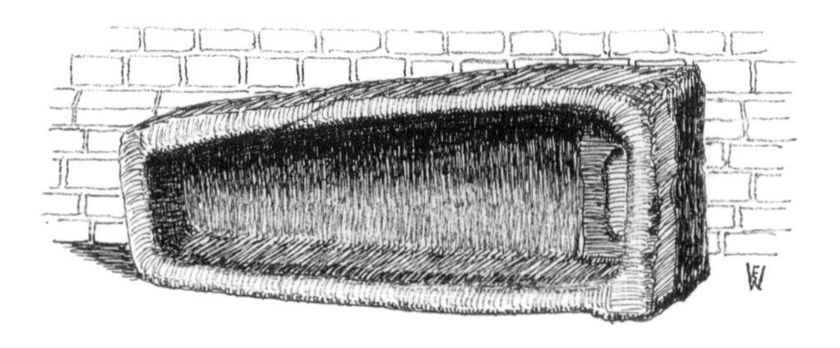

Stedham, St James

One mile west of Midhurst turn off the A272 to the north side of Stedham village, with its sandstone cottages, where the church stands close to the River Rother. There was a Saxon church on the site, built of local stone and having a central tower between nave and chancel. This was largely renovated by the Normans, the tower itself eventually being rebuilt in 1673. That is how it remained until 1850 when the nave and chancel were completely redesigned and rebuilt to the north of the tower. The line of the old building can be seen clearly on the tower to this day.

The visitor will find interest in the display at the back of the church – sketches of frescoes from the old church; early prayer books, one with a Service of Thanksgiving for deliverance from the Catholic Gunpowder Plot of 1605; a copy of the Geneva *Breeches Bible*, so named because of the translation of *Genesis 3* v7, 'They (Adam and Eve) sewed fig leaves together and made themselves breeches', printed in 1560. On the north side of the nave is a thirteenth century oak chest which was once used to secure church and parish documents.

Outside a pre-Saxon stone coffin and grave slabs can be seen, also an impressive yew tree said to pre-date the Christian faith. On the north side of the church is a dividing wall between the church and Stedham Hall. At one time the lord of the manor was patron of the church, but this responsibility has now passed to the Bishop of Chichester. The Hall itself has been divided into apartments managed by a property company, but the seventeenth-nineteenth century building remains a very fine sight.

STEDHAM HALL, MIDHURST.

BOXGROVE PRIORY

Boxgrove Priory

Turn off the A27 at the Boxgrove-Tangmere roundabout seven miles beyond Arundel, travelling west.

The Priory, though now a parish church, is by no means a typical country church. Built on the site of a Saxon church, soon after the Conquest, by monks from Lessay in Normandy, the building took on cathedral proportions. Originally the Benedictine monks used part of the building as their priory, making the rest of the building available to the local people to be used as their parish church. The twin dedication of the building to St Mary and St Blaise probably reflects this dual use of the complex. St Blaise was an Armenian bishop and physician. He became a recluse living in a cave befriending and healing animals. In the Roman persecutions under Licinius he was tortured with burning hot wool-carding combs and thrown into a lake. He survived only to be beheaded in 316AD, in spite of the toleration Edict of Milan in 313AD.

After the Dissolution of the Monasteries by Henry VIII the Priory section fell into disrepair, its ruins very evident today. The parishioners maintained the upkeep of their parish church section and the arrangement continues to the present time.

There is a wealth of historical and architectural interest to be gleaned. Sculptures, carvings, and beautiful stained glass abound, providing objective reminders of saints, Old Testament prophets, the Holy Family and teachings of Jesus.

A memorial window to the wife of Lord Lennox, killed by enemy action in London, June 1944, takes St Catherine of Alexandria as its subject. St Catherine is the patron saint of philosophers. At the tender age of eighteen she was an effective Christian apologist against the philosophers of the Emperor Maxentius. In the ongoing persecution of Christians the Emperor condemned her to die on a spiked wheel to which she was tied, but when the wheel began to turn it fell to pieces.

St Catherine of Alexandria

Imprisoned, she was visited by angels and when beheaded in 310AD it is said the angels carried her body to Mount Sinai.

Look for the ceiling boss and note how eight eyes have been placed to complete eight faces.

Boxgrove Priory's monastic ruins

ST. ANDREW, WEST STOKE

Eleventh century stonework frames a modern door

West Stoke, St Andrew

A warm bulky-looking church surrounded by trimmed yews in pleasant countryside near the Downs, two-and-a-half miles north west of Chichester.

Entrance is by the tower on the south side of the nave, the tower graced by a fifteenth century Sussex cap. Inside, immediately opposite in the north wall is the original Saxon entrance preserved by Norman and later restoration.

Visitors may like to have binoculars with them to take advantage of viewing the twelfth century mural behind the oak beam over the chancel arch; the framed details of the mural on the south wall of the nave give valuable information.

In the sanctuary an impressive monument of 1635 testifies to Adrian and Mary Stoughton and their sixteen children. The skulls in the hands of the children are a sombre remembrance of their dead brothers and sisters. Opposite in the sanctuary is a restored trefoil-headed piscina.

The east end lancet windows portray the theme of the Passion with the prayerful petition from the Prayer Book Litany, 'By thy Cross and Passion; Good Lord, deliver us'. Other memorial windows in the chancel depict the Saints George, Anne, Cecilia and Lucia, while the west window portrays The Good Shepherd.

In the churchyard an attractive cork oak adds pleasure, while the Cavendish memorial begs the question – why is it sited north to south while the other graves are in the usual east to west position?

A section of the 1635 memorial to Adrian and Mary Stoughton who had sixteen children

ST. MARY THE VIRGIN, SHIPLEY.

Family crest on the Burrell memorial plaque

Shipley, St Mary the Virgin

In pleasantly ordered pasture land, four miles west of Cowfold off the A272, the church of St Mary the Virgin stands close to the River Adur in the village of Shipley. The King's Windmill, prominent from the approach to the church, adds distinctly to the picturesque setting.

The large church,with its central tower to nave and chancel, is so obviously Norman. Inside the building the twin Norman arches under the tower present an impressive and dominant feature.

Linked with the Knights Templars in its twelfth century origins, the church has a very modern link with another organisation – the Scouting movement, indicated in the richly coloured window at the east end of the north aisle. The window was donated in 1984 by the 1st Shipley and Southwater Scouts to commemorate their first fifty years, and to give thanks for Robert Baden-Powell the founder of the Scouting movement. Among other windows the visitor will appreciate those by C E Kempe, the 'Master of Glass', and note the depiction of Shipley Mill (King's Windmill) in one of the south wall windows.

King's Mill from the church approach

ST. MARY, SENNICOTTS.

The Bowes-Lyon crest on the memorial to Captain Geoffrey Francis Bowes-Lyon

Sennicotts, St Mary

Two miles north-west of Chichester, off the Funtington Road, the church stands in isolation in the fields. Built in 1826 by Charles Baker, Lord of the Manor, the church was maintained independently until recently when it was placed under the pastoral care of Funtington.

The tower is embattled and the gables crow-stepped. An interesting architectural feature is immediately evident in the flint-chip garreting on the tower – garreting being the insertion of flint chippings into the mortar joints. A stairway in the tower leads to the west end gallery, and another door at the base of the tower opens into the single room of the chapel with its attractive white box pews, simple chandeliers and terracotta coloured walls.

There is a richly coloured east window which is original to the building, depicting Christian social caring on the theme of our Lord's words in *Matthew 25* v35: 'I was hungry and you gave me food, I was thirsty and you gave me drink, I was a stranger and you welcomed me, I was naked and you clothed me, I was sick and you visited me, I was in prison and you came to me.'

The Bowes-Lyon crest can be seen on the memorial to Captain Geoffrey Francis Bowes-Lyon, cousin to the late Queen Elizabeth the Queen Mother. The memorial has this challenging precept: 'Man is the creator of thought; what he thinks upon in this life that hereafter he becomes.'

Intending visitors to this delightful little church need to note that in the present climate of thefts and vandalism the church remains locked when unattended.

Box pews and benches

ST. MARY, BINSTED

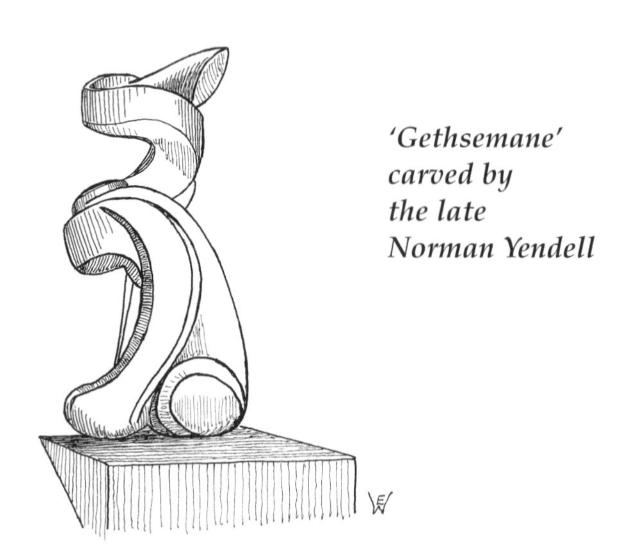

*'Gethsemane'
carved by
the late
Norman Yendell*

Binsted, St Mary

The quietness of this Norman church and surroundings, deep in luscious countryside two miles west of Arundel, is a benediction in itself, well worth savouring.

The extensive renovations of 1867 saw a gallery and ceiling removed, but a vestry and the delightful south porch were added.

Of particular interest are the faded murals in the splay of the Norman window – north wall interior. Only the stronger coloured pigments have survived, leaving incomplete designs; however, a helpful information sheet is provided alongside.

Murals depicting St Margaret of Scotland and a three-branched tree. The modern stained-glass features St Stephen

The three-branched tree may represent the Tree of Life, or the Holy Trinity. The unusual form of the tree may be intended as a respond to St Margaret opposite. As she is giving praise to God so creation praises its Creator, St Margaret of Scotland (1045-93). The mural was a tribute to the Saxon princess Margaret, granddaughter of Edmund Ironside. Margaret's brother Edgar failed in a rebellion against William the Conqueror, consequently the family fled to Scotland. Margaret eventually married Malcolm who became Malcolm III, King of Scotland. As his Queen, Margaret brought to bear a great deal of influence through her personal piety and dedication, assisting the poor, building churches, providing for pilgrims, and many other good works for which she was canonized in 1251.

A well-finished modern carving, 'Gethsemane', by the late Norman Yendell, represents the mystic aspect of Christ's agony in the Garden of Gethsemane. The kneeling in prayer. The grief. The indication of a chalice, spiralling from the apex of the carving, recall the verses of *St Matthew* ch26 v36-39.

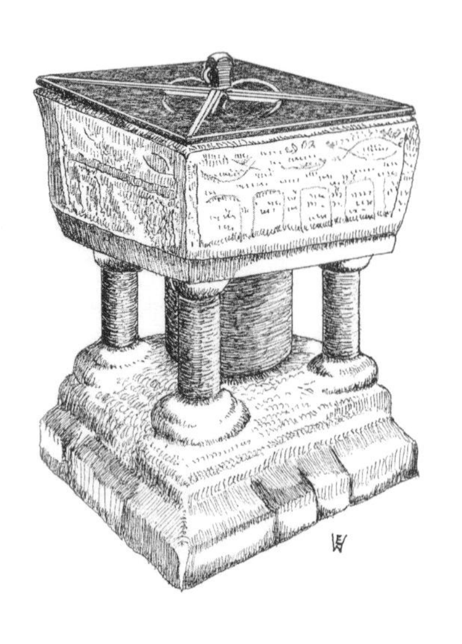

Norman font of Sussex marble

Barnham, St Mary

The approach to the church of St Mary is by Highground Lane to the imposing lych-gate atop the few steps and flanked by impressive yews and copper beech. This Norman church, mentioned in the *Domesday Book,* has been extensively repaired with brick and plaster but holds much interest with architectural features and windows ranging from the twelfth century to the twentieth century.

In the chancel a memorial sculpture of St Genevieve graces the sill of the south east window.

The Sussex marble font is Norman. On the worn grave slabs near the font the nineteenth century Murrell memorial describes death as a welcome palliative:

Afflictions sore long time I bore
Physicians were in vain,
Till death did seize and
God did please
To Ease me of my pain.

The white painted wooden bell-turret houses a single fourteenth century bell dedicated to St Mary.

At the west boundary gate in the churchyard an impressive view of Barnham Court is afforded. A superbly proportioned seventeenth century brick building with attractive dutch gables provided a subject this artist could not resist.

BARNHAM COURT.

ST. MARY, BEPTON.

Ninteenth century cast-metal headstone

Bepton, St Mary

Bell Lane runs parallel to the Downs from Cocking to the scattered cottages of Bepton. St Mary's is approached on the pathway from Church Farm when the huge Norman tower suddenly comes into view presenting an impressive edifice with its supporting seventeenth century buttresses.

Information in Peter Leicester's interesting church guide indicates that a Saxon church was built on the site by St Wilfrid's Community in 700AD, to be replaced in 1185 by the Normans. The church is mentioned in the *Domesday Book.*

The huge proportions of the tower apparently presented difficulties to the Norman builders because it began to tilt under the weight of the 3ft 6in thick walls, resulting in a greatly modified scheme brought to completion in the latter part of the thirteenth century. The massive clasp buttresses were added in 1620 to prepare for the addition of a second bell, and to counter the tower's south-west inclination.

Thirteenth century lancet windows in the chancel hold attractive nineteenth and twentieth century stained glass depicting Faith, Charity, Sanctus, St Wilfrid, and Angels by the Sepulchre. Alongside the vestry door, in the chancel, is a 7ft long ancient gravestone, carved with a Calvary Cross and four-gospel circles. The memorial is to Rado De La Hedol, probably an important Norseman of his day, but what he was and did remains unknown.

Victims of the Black Death (1349) lie in the churchyard in an unmarked mass-grave to the south-west of the tower under the shubbery. A number of graves are more unusually marked with cast-metal crosses bearing the three letter monogram, IHS, for 'Jesus'. Visitors will enjoy this sanctuary and its setting.

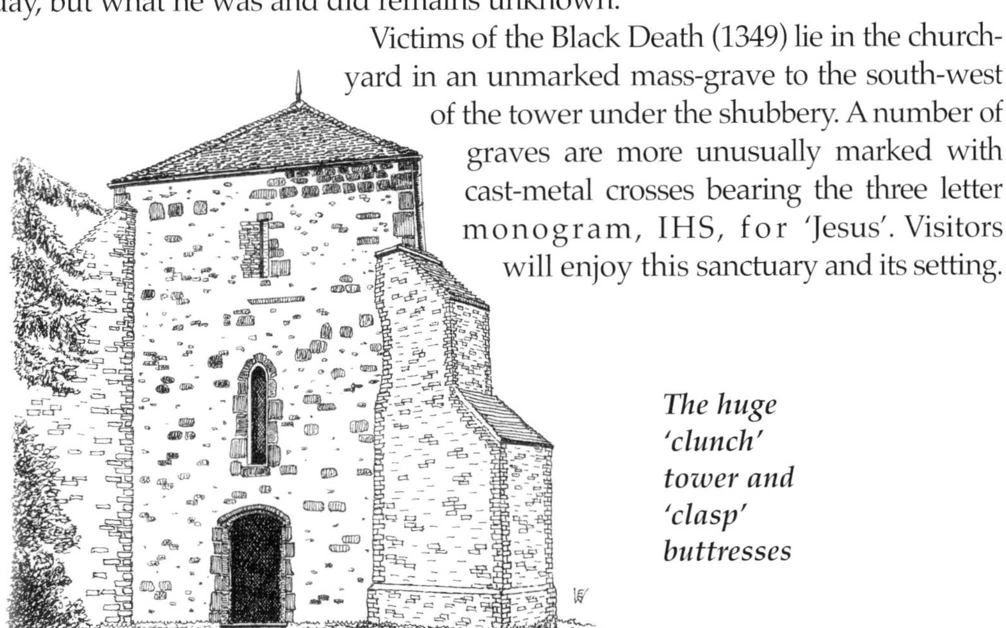

The huge 'clunch' tower and 'clasp' buttresses

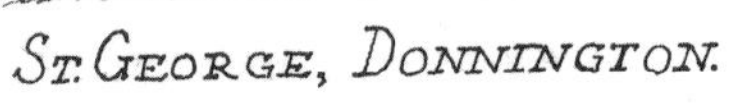

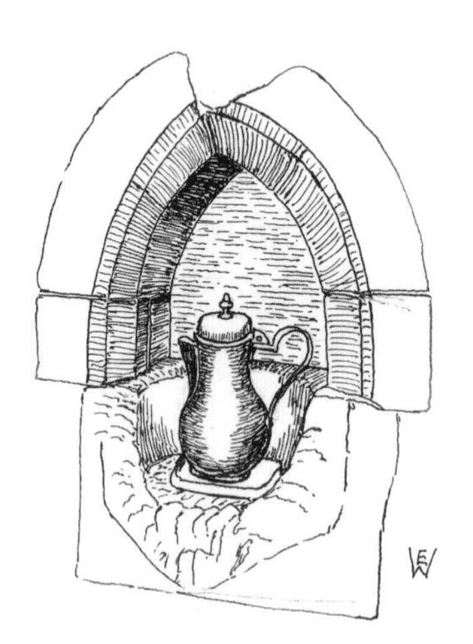

Copper ewer in the defaced water stoup

Donnington, St George

One mile south of Chichester on the Sidlesham to Selsey Road the church of St George stands in isolation close to the hamlet of Donnington. Turn off the road on to the access track across the field.

A Saxon building was replaced by the Normans and the embattled tower was added in the sixteenth century and now houses three bells. Extensive renovations were carried out by the Victorians, however, a fire severely damaged the nave and aisles in 1939, cruelly followed by bomb damage in 1941 when the windows of the chancel and Trinity Chapel were blown out. The replacement windows followed the Early English style, and the church was reopened in October 1942.

The clean lines of the twentieth century font provide a pleasant surprise. It was presented to the church by the Reverend A H M Kempe who was vicar of the parish from 1947 to 1963.

Impressive memorials to the Page and Crosbie families are to be seen in the Trinity Chapel, especially the alabaster busts, unnamed, on individual plinths.

The memorial to General Sir John Gustavus Crosbie, GCH, who died in August 1843, is a model of classically expressed care and respect:

Having honourably served his king and country, in the earlier part of his mortal career, he retired into private life where he fulfilled the duties of an affectionate husband and father, dying loved and respected by all who knew him, but more especially by his nine children who survive to deplore his loss.

The delights of a visit to this sanctuary will be added to if the visitor takes time to look across the fields to the fine spire of Chichester Cathedral.

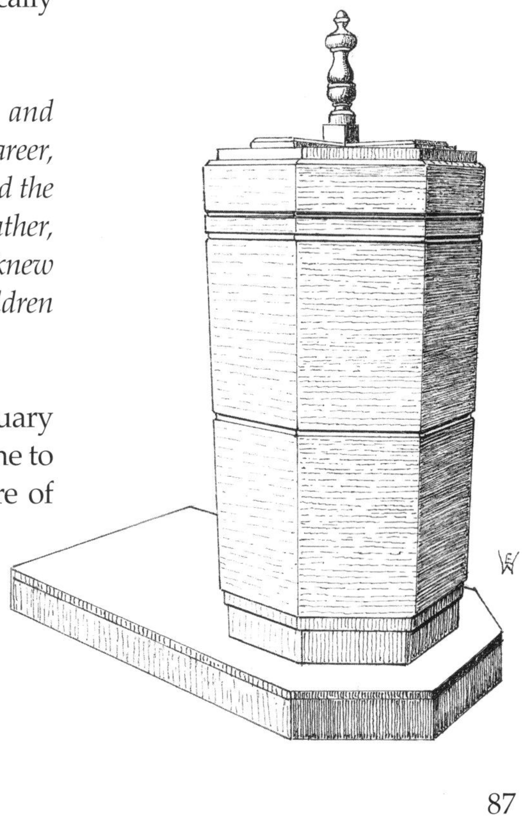

The strikingly modern font

St. Mary, East Lavant

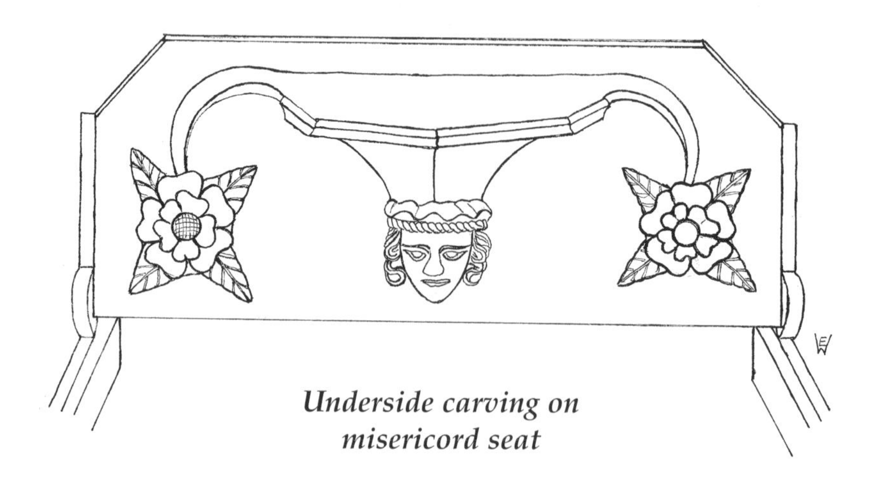

Underside carving on misericord seat

East Lavant, St Mary

The church stands on the rising ground on the north side of the village of East Lavant, two miles north of Chichester. Its dominant feature is the seventeenth century brick tower on the south aspect of the building. The west nave is part of the original twelfth century church, surprisingly not mentioned in the *Domesday Book*. The north aisle is thirteenth century; the chancel and part of the nave were rebuilt in the nineteenth century. Five misericords provide an attractive feature in the choir stalls; the underside carvings present interest and decoration when the seats are upturned.

There are many memorials to interest the visitor. Church folklore relates that the nail driven into the floor between the Compton memorial floor slabs was the defiant gesture of an atheist. Driven by drink he proclaimed his disclaimer in the church fulfilling his promise to hammer in the nail as evidence of his act late in the evening. Hammering in the nail he unfortunately pinned his smock so firmly he could not leave; darkness fell and in the morning he was found dead at the spot!

The nineteenth century stained glass windows are rich in colour and meaning. The west window depicts the theme of Resurrection in the raising of Lazarus and the Widow of Nain's son. The east window shows Christ in Ascension. There is a delicately-coloured memorial window in the stone-faced south chapel. Below this window, on the altar, the pelican sustaining her chicks with her own blood is a potent symbol of Christ's self-giving on the Cross.

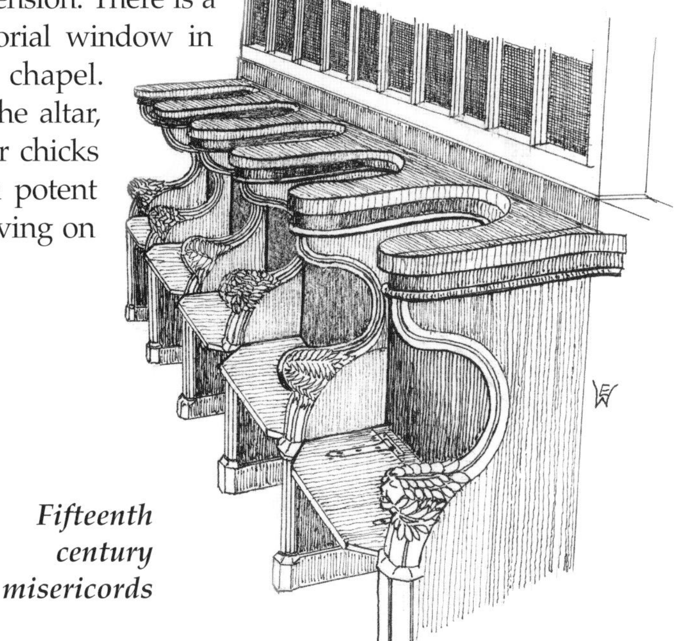

Fifteenth century misericords

ST. MICHAEL, AMBERLEY

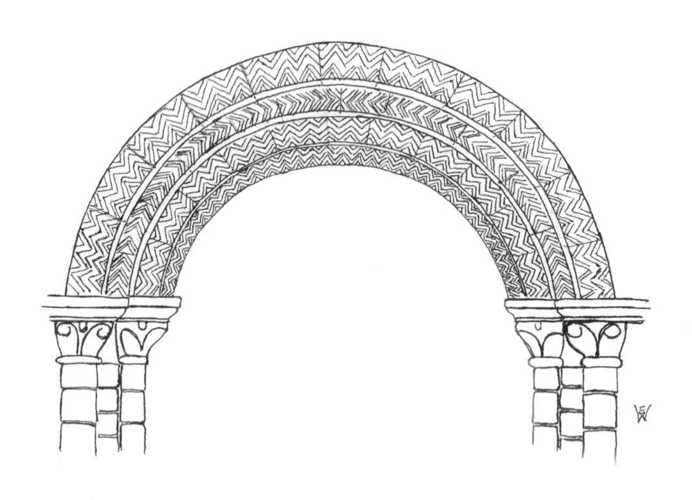

Late Norman chancel arch

Amberley, St Michael

Sandwiched between the fourteenth century castle and the village of Amberley, St Michael's church lays claim to having Bishop Luffa as its originator in 1100. (Bishop Ralph de Luffa succeeded to the see of Chichester in 1091 and immediately organised the establishment of the Cathedral Church in Chichester rather than Selsey. Building on the site of a Saxon church Bishop Luffa's Cathedral was dedicated in 1108.)

The south aisle and tower of St Michael's were added to the nave and chancel in 1230. A large chancel and aisle-less nave adequately balance the dominant features of the late-Norman chancel arch. The recently uncovered wall paintings alongside the chancel arch are thought to be from the same period as the arch, and depict scenes of the Crucifixion and Resurrection of Jesus. Interestingly the yellow borders to the panels are decorated with fish designs. The fish was the earliest symbol used by Christians.

East end lancet windows with wide splays span the width of the chancel making an effective reredos. Among a number of attractive stained-glass windows a modern, semi-circular window is immediately eye-catching. It has been fitted into the arch of the original Norman doorway on the north side of the nave.

The king-post roof timbers present an impressive feature in the nave and chancel. In addition to the fascinating architecture of the church, the visitor will surely be delighted by the many thatched buildings in the attractive village of Amberley.

One of many thatched buildings in the village

The insignia and coat-of-arms of Sir Stirling-Hamilton, engraved on the clear glass of his memorial window

Funtington, St Mary

To the north of the well-kept churchyard is an impressive yew tree said to be as old, if not older, than the church itself. The first record of a priest at St Mary's is 1174, when the church was under the care of Bosham.

North and south chapels were added in the thirteenth and fourteenth centuries and the tower in the fifteenth century. The strong Christian commitment of the Victorians brought the almost inevitable restorations on a major scale to St Mary's in the middle of the nineteenth century.

Of particular delight are the rich colours and design of the east end windows, another Victorian addition. In complete contrast are the memorial windows to Captain Sir Stirling-Hamilton. His coat-of-arms and family crest along with a tree are skilfully engraved on clear glass.

Many memorials to eminent people add a personal and historical perspective to reward the visitor.

Former water source preserved alongside the yew tree

The unusual 'open' pulpit

ST. ANDREW'S, STEYNING

Early twelfth century arcade in the north aisle, left; two of the forty-eight reredos Tudor panels, above

Steyning, St Andrew

From the village High Street turn at Lintott's Corner into the delightful Church Street leading to St Andrew's. The church was founded in the eighth century by Cuthman, a Sussex-born monk. Wherever his missionary endeavours took him, Cuthman caringly carried his paralysed mother, pulling her along in a couch-cart. When at last the cart broke at Steyning the saintly Cuthman took it as a divine directive and there he stayed to erect a hut for his mother and a church for the local dwellers. He was buried in the church he built, but on its replacement with a stone church after the Conquest, Cuthman's remains were transferred to the monastery at Fecamp, Normandy, in whose gift St Andrew's had been placed.

The chequered stone and flint west tower is a sixteenth century replacement of the original centrally placed Norman tower. Stone coffin lids in the porch are effective reminders of the church's Saxon links, particularly with St Cuthman and King Ethelwulf (father of King Alfred the Great) once buried at Steyning, later to be re-interred at Winchester.

St Cuthman is well remembered by the south aisle chapel dedicated to him and the colourful modern window by Ann Goodman. There is also a nineteenth century window in the south aisle depicting St Cuthman as a shepherd and church-builder, also he is pictured simply and effectively in a design for church kneelers.

Twelfth century cylindrical pillars and zigzag arches of the nave flank the early twelfth century chancel arch in truly impressive Romanesque style. Forty-eight carved oak Tudor panels form a fascinating reredos and complement the wagon-roof panels of the chancel. The inner porch door is Norman, as is the font.

St Andrew's is a must for visitors.

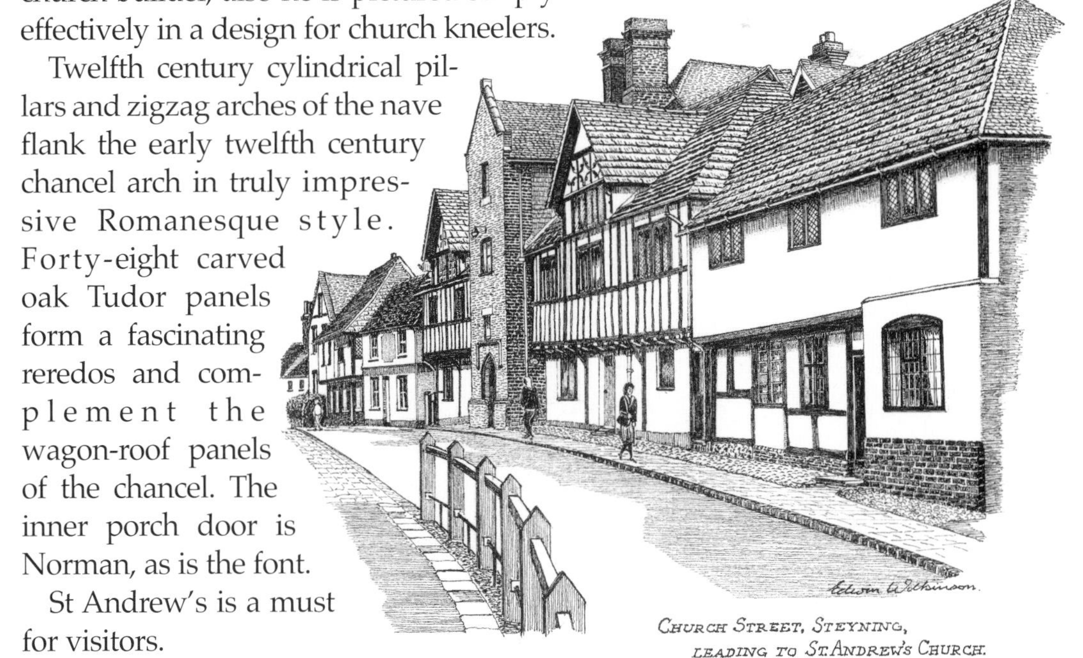

CHURCH STREET, STEYNING, LEADING TO ST. ANDREW'S CHURCH.

ST. MARY THE VIRGIN, SOMPTING.

The Abbot Stone

Sompting, St Mary the Virgin

The church stands on the north side of the A27 one mile east of Worthing, but if approached on the minor road from Steyning, glorious views of the Downs and coastal areas can be enjoyed.

The attractive and rare feature of St Mary's is immediately obvious in the Saxon tower with its Rhenish helm cap – a German architectural feature which is now unique among church towers in this country. At the base of the tower, inside, at the west end of the nave, fine examples of carved Saxon capitals are to be seen on the tower arch.

The north and south transepts were added by the Knights Templars early in the twelfth century, not as part of the whole but as separate chapels for the use of the Knights themselves. Apparently the high arch of the south transept doorway was proportioned to accommodate their raised banners, also in the south transept the Norman 'Abbot Stone' can be seen on the east wall.

Saxon capitals, west tower

Almost two centuries later the Knights Hospitallers replaced the Knights Templars and built a new chapel on the north side of the tower, at the same time opening the north and south chapels to access by the public from the body of the church, creating the north and south transepts of the church as it is today.

When the Knights Hospitallers were disbanded during the reign of Henry VIII their chapel fell into ruins but has been cleverly and effectively turned into a parish meeting room, opened in 1971.

There is a delightful east window depicting the Ascension of our Lord, and a beautifully carved limestone reredos, both of great merit and Victorian.

There are other carved Saxon stones on display and interesting memorials, but the visitor will be left with an abiding appreciation of that remarkable Saxon tower with its Rhenish helm.

Tillington, All Hallows

One mile west of Petworth on the A272 turn into the hamlet where the church, with its twelfth century origins, has become prominent with the addition of the impressive nineteenth century tower and its Scots Crown pinnacle. A persistent tradition holds that the artist Turner, an architect by training and closely linked with the church, suggested the design of the tower when Lord Egremont was planning a replacement tower and extensive renovation work which began in 1807. This comprehensive building work included adding the north aisle, extending the length of the chancel, providing the east window and the homely dormer windows to give added light in the nave.

The lower chamber of the tower doubles for a south transept in which stone steps from the original tower remain. The steps were used to gain access to the upper part of the heavy rood screen which was removed in the sixteenth century in deference to the changing trends in worship at that time.

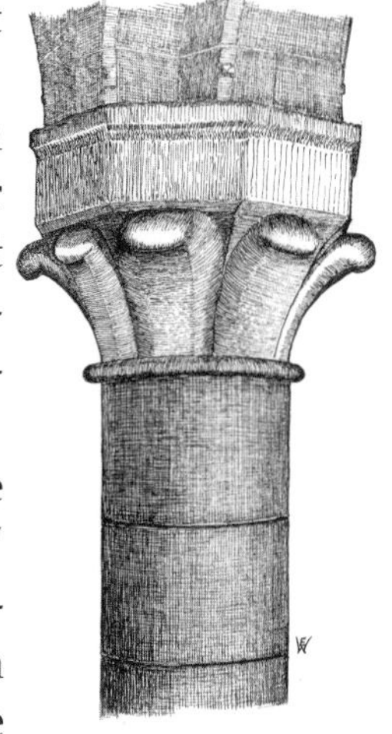

Thirteenth century palm leaf capitals

Among the many interesting memorials is a rather rare brass Crimean War memorial to 'Four Natives of the Parish' who died during the conflict in 1855. A genuine horse-plough, placed in the north aisle, is a fitting memorial in a farming community. Other noteworthy items include the font, which survives from the original Norman building, and the 600-year-old parish chest in the north aisle. The minstrel-angels window in the south aisle is inspirational.

The churchyard affords an advantageous view of the Horse Guards Inn, immediately opposite, linked with the famous regiment and the Napoleonic Wars.

THE HORSE GUARDS INN,
FROM THE CHURCHYARD

St. John the Evangelist, Bury.

Exterior water stoup

Bury, St John the Evangelist

A church of Early English style situated at the lower end of the village of Bury, close to the River Arun. Its large shingle-covered spire presents a dominant and attractive feature along with rendered walls and Horsham stone slab roofing over the south aisle.

Basically the building is twelfth century with the addition of a fifteenth century south porch, and nineteenth century restoration of the chancel. The roof was lowered and the spire added to the existing tower in 1603. Inside,two large pillars support the sweep of the roof to the south wall. A striking feature is the beautifully panelled chancel with the exquisitely carved reredos depicting the Nativity scene. The altar-table panels show Christ the Good Shepherd, the Pelican symbol and, unusually, an eagle killing a viper, this latter symbolic of St John the Evangelist's triumphant Gospel message over the powers of Satan.

Reredos carving of St Christopher

The carved figure of St Christopher is captured in typical pose carrying the increasingly heavy Christ-child across the storm riven swollen river. It was commonly believed that if anyone looked on an image of St Christopher they would not die that day; hence the Saint's continuing popularity in this age of increasing worldwide travel. St Christopher the man was a pagan ferryman, converted to Christ, and martyred for his faith during the Roman persecutions of Christians in the third century AD.

The nineteenth century east window gloriously depicts the Ascension of Jesus with angels and disciples in attendance.

This is an interesting church in a delightful setting, well worth a visit.

Fifteenth century font and thirteenth century pillar

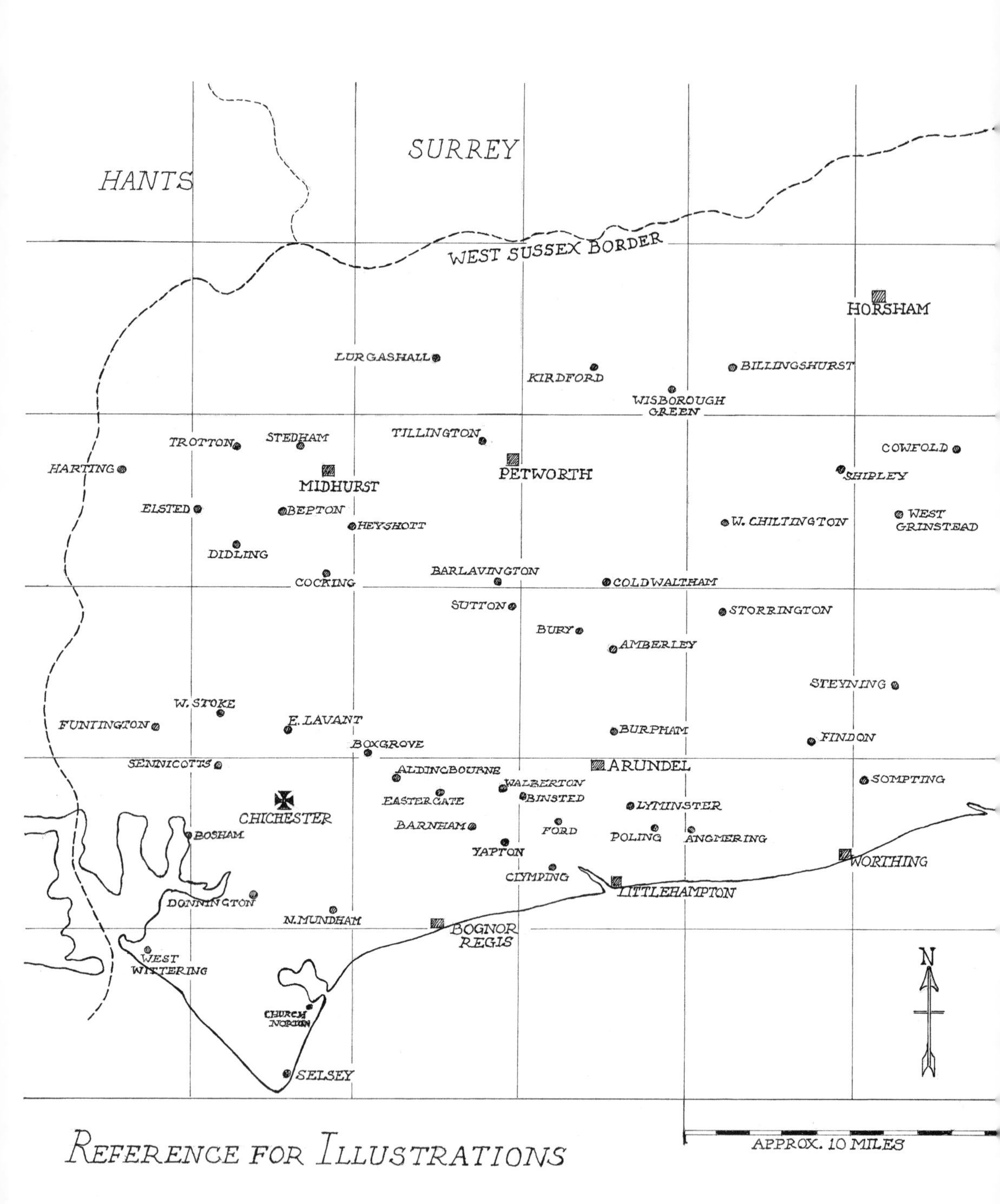

REFERENCE FOR ILLUSTRATIONS